Alberta

THE CHANGE FACTOR
The Risks and Joys

Other Books by Gary W. Kuhne
> The Dynamics of Discipleship Training
> The Dynamics of Faithful Living
> The Dynamics of Personal Follow-Up

THE CHANGE FACTOR

The Risks and Joys

GARY W. KUHNE

PYRANEE BOOKS

Zondervan Publishing House
Grand Rapids, Michigan

The Change Factor

This is a Pyranee Book
Published by the Zondervan Publishing House
1415 Lake Drive, S.E., Grand Rapids, Michigan 49506

Copyright © 1986 by The Zondervan Corporation

Library of Congress Cataloging in Publication Data

Kuhne, Gary W.
    The change factor.

    "Pyranee books."
    Includes bibliographies.
    1. Christian life—1960–   . I. Title.
BV4501.2.K767   1986   248.4   85-26530
ISBN 0-310-27251-3

All Scripture quotations, unless otherwise noted, are taken from *The Holy Bible: New International Version* (North American Edition). Copyright © 1973, 1978, 1984 by the International Bible Society. Used by permission of Zondervan Bible Publishers.

All rights reserved. No part of this publication may be reproduced, stored in a retrieval system, or transmitted in any form or by any means—electronic, mechanical, photocopy, recording, or any other—except for brief quotations in printed reviews, without the prior permission of the publisher.

Edited and designed by James E. Ruark

Printed in the United States of America

86 87 88 89 90 91 / 10 9 8 7 6 5 4 3 2 1

Contents

Preface : 7
1 : Is Change Really Possible? : 9
2 : Coping and Legalism: Dead Ends : 23
3 : "Secrets" and Self-Denial: Dead Ends : 37
4 : God's Formula for Change : 59
5 : Faith and Fullness : 77
6 : Faith and Sin : 99
7 : Obeying in Our Hearts and Minds : 113
8 : Obeying in Our Behavior : 129

Preface

This is a book about change in the Christian life and how God brings us into true conformity to the image of Christ. I am sure that many will wonder why I thought it necessary to write a book on an issue that has been addressed so frequently throughout the years by many capable writers.

As a defense of my action I confess I approached this topic very reluctantly. After going through some extremely difficult trials that revealed my own inadequacies in both strength and understanding, I began to recognize that I had misunderstood some very foundational issues regarding what it means to trust completely in Christ for strength. These misunderstandings, I have come to believe, are shared by many sincere Christians. This book is my attempt to correct these misunderstandings. Paul's statement in 2 Corinthians 1:8–9 mirrored my own trials and discoveries.

> We were under great pressure, far beyond our ability to endure, so that we despaired even of life. Indeed, in our hearts we felt the sentence of death. But this happened that we might not rely on ourselves but on God, who raises the dead.

THE CHANGE FACTOR

I too needed to come to the point of relying totally on God, and He allowed circumstances beyond my ability to endure to bring me to that point of dependence. Each of us needs to understand our true powerlessness before we will begin to rely totally on God instead of ourselves.

The concept of coming to the end of ourselves and the beginning of Christ-dependency is the essence of how one finds growth and lasting change in the Christian life. I have attempted to make a fresh statement of the dynamics of such Christ-dependency in terms understandable to the contemporary Christian community.

It is my prayer that you, the reader, will be led to a more practical understanding and appropriation of Christ as your strength and life. If you find within yourself a movement of heart to become free of self-reliance and to begin a life of Christ-dependency, I will feel my time has been worthwhile. May God minister to you as you read this volume.

◆ ONE ◆

Is Change Really Possible?

Much time, money, and energy is spent seeking change. From the crowded offices of psychiatrists and psychologists, to the endless mill of books and articles, to the rapid growth of Eastern mysticism and Transcendental Meditation, to the cosmetic industry's advertising for new breath, body odor, and hair color, we find modern man on a ceaseless quest for change. To add up the hours, effort, and finances expended in this quest nearly defies computation by mind or machine. Such a quest is not in any sense limited to unbelievers. We in the Christian community have not demonstrated a distinctively different mentality than the world around us.

Let's be honest with ourselves for a moment.

THE CHANGE FACTOR

Who hasn't spent time on New Year's Eve in introspection, evaluating their life and progress over the recent past? Such a time of evaluation offers an excellent opportunity for writing resolutions and turning over a "new leaf" or two. In fact, often the turning over of "new leaves" begins to resemble a woods in autumn.

Perhaps, as you reflect upon the recent past, a number of troublesome thoughts come to mind. Perhaps you realize, with hesitant honesty, that you are contemplating many of the same weaknesses that were the focus of previous resolutions. It would seem that no matter how much we desire change or how deeply we are motivated, some problem areas in our lives are never resolved. Troublesome attitudes and embarrassing actions have dogged our every step, year after frustrating year. How do we accomplish real change in our lives? How can we experience true transformation that goes beyond the merely superficial?

Everyone has had the experience of wishing they could start afresh in various areas of their lives. As Christians we should discover an even more intense desire for change within our hearts than the natural man. Having been made new creations through the rebirth that accompanies repentance and faith, we discover deep within ourselves a strong inclination to align with the righteous life revealed in the written and living Word. Whenever we find ourselves consistently failing to live in harmony with this inclination,

IS CHANGE REALLY POSSIBLE?

we become frustrated and miserable, out of peace with both ourselves and God. Such misery breeds a deep motivation for achieving true and lasting change in our daily Christian experience.

In spite of our universal longings for growth, the means to permanent change seem to remain hopelessly hidden for untold numbers of sincere people. The answers most frequently encountered in the quest for change seem ambiguous and contradictory. The Christian who studies the Bible finds a lifestyle described that seems at best idealistic and at worst a cruel impossibility. Many Christians find, as years pass, increasing spiritual discouragement and stagnation. Many then settle for a spiritual life that is far from fulfilling and satisfying. With such a tragic outcome, the issue of change can be seen as one of the most important concerns we will ever face in this life.

It is important that Christians find their way out of these spiritual blahs. Does God really intend that we will change? I believe Scripture offers an understandable answer to this question, and it is a resounding "yes." The Bible promises that we can find true change, i.e., *the progressive transformation over time of a person's characteristic ways of thinking, feeling, and acting.* In theological terms such "change" is called "sanctification."

The principles of real change are able to be discovered in the clear teachings of God's Word. God does have a way He intends to use to gradually bring each of His children into growing conformity with the image of His Son, our Lord Jesus Christ. Yet I am also convinced that many Christians must undergo a major renewal in their mindset before God's answer to change can be understood and appropriated.

The Scriptures clearly show that God's thoughts are not man's thoughts, nor His ways man's ways (Isa. 55:8). Attempting to understand how to change, without first consulting God and His Word, will inevitably produce wrong answers. These wrong answers create a confusing set of deceptions that lead many people astray from God's way. These errors, masquerading as truth, must be unmasked and revealed as dead ends in the quest for change. Not only will man's answers never result in real change, but many are actually harmful to the unsuspecting person. Recognizing these errors is the kind of mind-renewal to which I am referring and must precede any real understanding of God's solutions. We should not be surprised to discover that God's avenue for change is different from what we expect.

Although we find God's answer for change throughout the Word of God, I believe that chapters 2 and 3 of Paul's Epistle to the Colossians most clearly explains the dynamics of achieving true personal transformation. This passage presents the answer in a manner Christians today can readily grasp. By studying these two chapters we will discover how Paul reveals the

IS CHANGE REALLY POSSIBLE?

presuppositions and mechanics of growth and change in the Christian life. In the process of accomplishing this goal, Paul also exposes the most common deceptions involved in sanctification. He shows how these deceptions both discourage sincere believers and direct human energy toward methods that are ultimately unproductive.

The initial chapters of this book will focus on the deceptions, showing them to be dead ends in the process of transformation. After accomplishing this mental house cleaning, we will be ready to turn attention to the true dynamics of change. Before examining the deceptions, however, Paul sets the stage by stating a number of crucial presuppositions. These truths form a foundation for understanding change, growth, and transformation in the Christian life.

> We proclaim him, admonishing and teaching everyone with all wisdom, so that we may present everyone perfect in Christ. To this end I labor, struggling with all his energy, which so powerfully works in me. . . . My purpose is . . . that they may have the full riches of complete understanding, in order that they may know the mystery of God, namely, Christ, in whom are hidden all the treasures of wisdom and knowledge. I tell you this so that no one may deceive you by fine-sounding arguments.
> (Colossians 1:28–29; 2:2–4)

In these verses from Colossians, Paul provides the foundation and the framework on

THE CHANGE FACTOR

which the biblical answer for change and personal transformation is built. He states five presuppositions in these verses that set the stage for understanding the process. Let's examine each of these presuppositions.

CHANGE IS POSSIBLE

The first presupposition is the fact that change is really possible. Paul teaches this when he states that his goal is "to present everyone mature [perfect] in Christ." Apparently change and growth into the image of Christ is indeed God's clear intention for all believers.

I believe it is important to establish this principle at the outset of this book. Without seeing God's intentions, the whole quest for change could be dismissed as a project rooted in pure human idealism. The goal of growing into conformity to the image of Christ did not originate in the mind of someone enamored with impractical idealism or utopian fantasies. Rather, it was God Himself, speaking through Paul, the tireless missionary apostle, who articulated this challenge.

We are not being challenged to find what doesn't exist. God is not playing a cruel game with our hopes, planning to keep us always frustrated. Instead, God is promising a progressive personality transformation achievable by all who obediently seek it.

IS CHANGE REALLY POSSIBLE?

WE BOTH HAVE A ROLE

The second presupposition refers to a paradox in Christian living. In verse 29 Paul makes the apparently contradictory statement that *he labors with God's energy!* In other words, Paul says that *he* does something and at the same time *God* is doing it through him. How can such a statement be true? To understand this is to understand the basics behind true personal growth.

What Paul is showing us is the delicate balance God intends to characterize our Christian lives. Although we will examine this paradoxical balance later in this book, we should spend a moment thinking about implications of all this for the issue of change. This apparent paradox is encountered often in the Scripture. For example:

> *Therefore, my dear friends, as you have always obeyed—not only in my presence, but now much more in my absence—continue to work out your salvation with fear and trembling, for it is God who works in you to will and to act according to his good purpose.*
> (Philippians 2:12–13)
>
> *I have been crucified with Christ and I no longer live, but Christ lives in me. The life I live in the body, I live by faith in the Son of God, who loved me and gave himself for me.*
> (Galatians 2:20)
>
> *We pray this in order that you may live a life worthy of the Lord . . . being strengthened with all power according to his glorious might. . . .*
> (Colossians 1:10–11)

THE CHANGE FACTOR

These verses and others stress this paradox of "I do" and "God does." This paradox is a crucial concept, and we can fall into serious error if we don't keep these truths in proper balance. The error can arise from either direction.

We can go out of balance by focusing on our role and conclude that changes comes when we grit our teeth and work out the obedience God desires to see in our own strength. Such self-effort ultimately leads to discouragement and failure. We can also go out of balance by focusing too much on God's role and forgetting our own. Such an error will breed an unhealthy passivity in our Christian living. This passivity will also lead to discouragement and failure.

We must keep *both* truths in balance if the paradox is to yield the product of change in our lives.

CHRIST IS KEY

The third presupposition pertains to the role Christ plays in change. Paul demonstrates in these verses that the true resource for the task of growth is Jesus Christ Himself, the "mystery of God." It is Christ who provides the answer for change. The important role Christ plays in the process of growth will be developed at length later in this book. It is sufficient now merely to say that Christ is the key we are seeking in finding change.

An unfortunate preoccupation has come to exist in segments of the Christian community in our day. Focus on the *true source* of change, Jesus Christ, has been replaced by focus on the Holy Spirit. This is primarily due to the confusion many feel regarding the role of Christ and the role of the Holy Spirit. The Scriptures clearly explain that Jesus Christ lives His resurrection life in and through us in the power of the Holy Spirit. It is the Holy Spirit's role to minister the life of Christ within us. In the process of this ministry, the Holy Spirit seeks to focus attention and glory on the source of life, Jesus Christ Himself.

All too frequently the interest of Christians is in the Spirit *instead* of the One He came to glorify. This misplaced focus has led people to a preoccupation with the Spirit instead of the Son and has made Christ's role in our daily walk an all but meaningless issue.

To be told Christ is our answer is of little use unless we are also given understanding as to how He works and how we are to respond. Paul was not giving us meaningless clichés in these chapters. He unfolds clearly, under inspiration of the Spirit, the dynamics of Christ-centered growth and change. Paul shows us the "riches and treasure" that are found only in Christ Himself. This teaching naturally leads to presupposition four.

WE CAN UNDERSTAND

The fourth presupposition is that God wants us to have complete understanding regarding growth and change in the Christian life. He promises this in Colossians 2:2. This understanding is granted for the purpose of knowing Christ, "the mystery of God."

A Christian doesn't need to be confused about growth and change. If we are struggling with confusion about how Christ can make the real difference in us, then we must admit that the fault is not God's. He has spoken completely and adequately about just such concerns.

God's intention to give us "complete understanding" doesn't imply that we will gain something similar to omniscience. Only God is omniscient. Rather, the promise is that we will gain adequate knowledge regarding how to achieve the goal of knowing Christ. That knowledge will then lead to change because Christ, as we have already noted, is the key to change. God's promise is not an empty one.

DECEPTION IS POSSIBLE

In the last presupposition, Paul warns us that deceptions abound when we seek the means to personal change and growth. Paul had a deep sense of concern for other believers and sought to protect the ones he loved from these deceptions.

The implication in Colossians 2 is that deception was already taking place within the Colossian church. We also face many deceptive "answers" in our day. Thus we can relate closely to the Colossian believers in these things, although we are separated from them by culture and eighteen centuries.

Deception is no respecter of motive. We encounter deception as quickly from those with good motives as we do from those with bad ones. Deception can come by design or through innocence. We need a foundation for truth that rises above the intentions and motives behind men's teachings. We need the foundation provided by God's Word to be delivered from deception and to find lasting safety.

In large part our susceptibility to deception is rooted in our deep desires for lasting change. Burdened down with our sins, failures, and sense of inadequacies, we are vulnerable to anyone offering the possibility of deliverance.

A key to understanding the errors Paul describes is to realize that these deceptions will usually sound quite convincing. The passage says these positions stem from "fine-sounding arguments." Thus it is clear we are focusing on issues that demand far more than a cursory glance to understand their inadequacy.

If we were approached by someone offering an answer that was plainly illogical and inconsistent, we could easily dismiss the entire position as nonsense and go on our way unaffected. However, if we are approached by a sympathetic individual who offers an answer that makes a lot of sense, the position is not able to be dismissed quite so easily. Instead, we are far more apt to listen and begin to build hope for change upon the "truth" presented. So we are drawn deeper and deeper into the deception and ultimately set up for a fall. When the system doesn't fulfill its promises, our hopes are dashed.

Because these deceptions further damage already hurting lives, Paul's ministry included a fair amount of demolition. He was committed to destroying "fine-sounding arguments" wherever he encountered them. His goal was to expose the deceptions as ultimately unbiblical and therefore untrue. We can see this attitude at work in Paul's second epistle to the Corinthian church.

> We demolish arguments and every pretension that sets itself up against the knowledge of God, and we take captive every thought to make it obedient to Christ.
>
> (2 Corinthians 10:5)

Deception inevitably sets itself up against the truth of God and His Word. Paul was committed to demolishing arguments (answers) that were false because they ultimately would become strong opposition to the truth.

We must recognize this dynamic. Deception undermines the truth of God and His Word. Deception never remains simply an issue of abstract intellectual discussion; it always leads to disobedience to the will of God. A false answer ultimately prevents a Christian from gaining the knowledge of God he so desires and, as a result, prevents the deliverance God promises to provide for His children.

Recognizing the danger of deceptions, we now turn our attention to Colossians 2 in which Paul unmasks four important deceptions. These deceptions, or "dead ends," are coping, legalism, secrets, and self-denial.

◆ TWO ◆

Coping and Legalism: Dead Ends

See to it that no one takes you captive through hollow and deceptive philosophy, which depends on human tradition and the basic principles of this world rather than on Christ.

(Colossians 2:8)

At the beginning of this book I noted that concern for change is not limited to the Christian. The nonbeliever is also desperately seeking to be delivered from his own weaknesses. It should not be surprising, therefore, to discover that the world around us has come up with its own answers to this human quest.

When I use the word "world," I am referring to the culture and perspectives of the unsaved community. This is the usual meaning in

Scripture when the word "world" is used as a translation of the Greek word *kosmos*. Our human culture surrounds us and attempts to conform us to its views. This subtle pressure to conform is clearly seen in the question of how to change.

The world around us offers a bewildering array of "answers" that have arisen from the untold dollars and efforts expended annually in research and therapy. Amid a vast array of answers, close study reveals a common denominator. Ultimately they all stress that the answer to change lives within people themselves. There are differences in perspective regarding the source of problems and the specific steps to be taken to solve them, but the idea of looking within for solutions is universal to all. Man is exhorted to look within himself for the solution to change.

Paul warns us that these worldly solutions will lead to a form of enslavement. Isn't it ironic that the very answers offered to gain deliverance result in bondage? The Greek word translated "captivity" in the New International Version is the word *sulagogeo*. The word means to be carried off as booty or spoils of war, or to be led into slavery. The concept communicated is quite a serious one. The world's answers are not simply a harmless deception, but become a trap for a believer. We can find ourselves enslaved by the very means through which we had hoped to find redemption.

This paradox should not surprise the believer. Being harmed instead of helped by the world is inevitable when we realize that this world is the product of the master of deception, Satan. When we are led to accept as true and adequate an answer that is neither, we will end up centering our lives around a faulty hub. Such solutions will lead to the establishment of life patterns that are counterproductive in facing the real difficulties of living.

The concept that the answer to change lies within man himself leads inevitably to self-reliance. This self-reliance is the common denominator of all secular attitudes toward change. Such self-reliance is expressed most clearly by seeking the strength within to cope with life. This truth in turn results in the world's solutions, when reduced to their most basic form, being limited to simply learning to cope.

Because we are incapable of bringing true change, looking within is a futile search unless our definition of success is redefined. With ourselves as our only resources, the best we can hope for is to cope more effectively with our selves or our circumstances. In any case, our standard for success must be conveniently removed from any relationship to real change. Instead of becoming *different*, the emphasis must be upon becoming *adjusted*. As a result, many therapy models can demonstrate a certain degree of success in achieving such a limited goal.

Yet the question must be asked, "Is that all there is?" Is learning to cope with life a legitimate and adequate goal for a Christian? We are certainly happy and thankful when someone who has been suffering becomes able to adjust more successfully to life. This coping is commendable. Yet the question remains: Is coping synonymous with, or a subtle substitute for, change in the Christian life?

In observing those who have sought help through the world's answers it is not unusual for us to find many who show an increased ability to cope with life more effectively. Yet there is seldom a corresponding change in the inner man. Whatever has been accomplished is predominantly external, a shuffling around of habits and behaviors, a gaining of better methods of conflict resolution, or similar outcomes. The end result is the ability to live some degrees more effectively in this world without resorting to real change.

I am convinced that this external dynamic causes many people to stop short of the more significant change that God desires to produce in the inner man. Settling for an ability to cope as a substitute for transformation creates the perpetual captivity that Paul warns against. To stop short of change enslaves us to the person we were and prevents the personal freedom that comes from discovering the person God intends us to become. For the world's purposes, behavior, not the heart, is the focus of change. God's interest is first the heart and then the external behavior.

COPING AND LEGALISM: DEAD ENDS

We could perhaps understand the dangers inherent in the world's approach if we could see it as a type of vaccination. A similar virus is injected in order to build up a resistance to the real disease. The world's solutions vaccinate us against real change by offering us the ability to cope. This ability then makes us immune to change and produces complacency in us.

It is really not too difficult to understand why the world focuses on coping instead of change. Jeremiah wrote the following evaluation thousands of years ago, yet it remains the definitive statement of the core of the world's problem.

> *The heart is deceitful above all things and beyond cure. Who can understand it?*
> (Jeremiah 17:9)

The heart of a man lies outside the concern of the world specifically because it is "beyond cure." This results in the world's focusing its efforts on coping and external behaviors. Heart change or curing lies solely in the realm of divine activity. That activity is limited to those who look to God to provide what He promises in both salvation and Christian growth. Consider God's promise:

> *I will give you a new heart and put a new spirit in you; I will remove from you your heart of stone and give you a heart of flesh.*
> (Ezekiel 36:26)

THE CHANGE FACTOR

The world's methods are a dead end because they stop short of heart change and settle for increased ability to cope.

The second idea at the core of the world's solutions also grows out of the common denominator of self-reliance. Because of self-reliance, the answers never rest on Christ. The hub of a solution becomes changed environment, learned behaviors, or medication. Success, as defined by the world, is never dependent upon Christ. Yet Paul emphasizes a christocentric solution in Colossians and elsewhere in the New Testament. The diagnostic question becomes, "Does the solution being presented depend on Christ for the process of change?"

A solution that doesn't rest on the ministry of our Lord Jesus Christ is ultimately a worldly answer regardless of its religious veneer. When Christ is absent from a solution or is offered as an afterthought, the only means of real heart change has been rejected. The focus inevitably reduces to coping.

Coping is inadequate as an answer because its rationality is rooted in and dependent on the world's viewpoints and perceptions. Paul identifies this foundation in Colossians 2:8 as "hollow ... philosophy,... human tradition and the basic principles of this world." By this terminology Paul seeks to show that the principle of coping is rooted in systems of thinking built on the world's presuppositions instead of on divine revelation. In other words, coping as a solution originates with man, not God.

COPING AND LEGALISM: DEAD ENDS

The error of coping is not seen in its faulty logic or inconsistency. The error is found in the presuppositions underlying the logic. The presuppositions behind coping are faulty. Coping is based on faulty assumptions regarding the nature of man's problems. Man's problem lies deeper than merely his behaviors. Change, therefore, must involve more than modifying our behavior. We behave badly because our hearts are bad. Coping seeks to compensate for a bad heart instead of changing it.

The Holy Spirit, through Paul, warns Christians to be careful, aware that they can be drawn into captivity through reliance on compensating instead of changing. We should recognize that captivity is possible when a degree of relief is gained from the world's answers. Coping, at best, results in little more than a patch-up job in our lives. God is not interested in changing our ability to cope, but rather in enabling us, through true change in our hearts and minds, to respond differently to the world around us. The world leaves us the same inside and works to change our external behaviors or the environment in which we live. But God works within so that we respond differently because we *are* different.

I believe it is critical that we recognize that many people will find a degree of help from the world's solutions. Christians have a tendency to believe that if a system or solution isn't the total truth, then there is nothing of value in it at all. This tendency causes the Christian answer to be rejected as being out of touch with reality. Much wisdom can be gained by the unregenerate man through careful study and observation.

Insight into human behavior and problems can certainly be found in secular research. The problem is that apart from the divine revelation, the world cannot ultimately understand the true nature of man and his deepest problems. Lacking this revelation, the world's solutions are inadequate in their presuppositions and are therefore unable to change our hearts.

No heart change is possible if Christ is not central to the solution. Merely including Christ's name does not make something a true solution. Often Christ is added as an afterthought to make a human solution more palatable to the Christian community. A good test would be to mentally cross out all the references to Christ in a given solution. If this exercise results in no practical difference in the answer offered, than clearly the solution does not depend on Christ. God's answer to change will always involve Christ and be dependent on His power to bring about a solution.

LEGALISM

> *Therefore do not let anyone judge you by what you eat or drink, or with regard to a religious festival, a New Moon celebration or a Sabbath day. These are a shadow of the things that were to come; the reality, however, is found in Christ.*
> (Colossians 2:16–17)

COPING AND LEGALISM: DEAD ENDS

The second dead end Paul exposes in Colossians 2 is legalism. In the quest for true and lasting change, we are certain to encounter people who believe change comes through some form of religious legalism. The problem is an age-old conflict for the people of God. In its most basic form, legalism teaches that by abstaining from certain practices and exercising consistency in other practices, eventually we will become different people, changed in our hearts.

Legalism focuses on external behavior. The concept behind legalism can be summarized this way: We are made holy or kept from being holy by external practices. This is the essence of the answer to change offered by religious legalists.

Christians face constant pressure to view change and sanctification from this legalistic perspective. The pressure arises, as Paul shows, from the fact that external behaviors often become the focus of judgmental attitudes within the body of Christ. Since no one enjoys criticism, many Christians will allow themselves to be pressured into conformity to avoid it. As a result, external behaviors can become over significant in the Christian community.

The fallacy of legalism is exposed when we understand that it is not what goes into a man that makes him clean or unclean. Change and holiness grow from the inside out, not from the outside in. Holiness doesn't occur in our lives in the same way nutrients enter a plant.

THE CHANGE FACTOR

Through osmosis a plant absorbs food through its root system, allowing movement of external nutrients to internal cells. Change in man works in the opposite direction. True growth and change begin in the center of our personhood (the heart) and move from there to the surface, affecting our behavior. To understand this crucial truth is to understand the deception of legalism as an answer for change.

The belief that we can be made holy through external practices has subtly corrupted God's people throughout history. Christ aggressively confronted this mentality throughout His public ministry. A good example of such a confrontation is related in Matthew 15. In response to the Pharisees' defense of religious traditions, Jesus declares that God's Word overrules their traditions, and He then rebukes them for their misguided confidence in legalism.

Jesus' words left no doubt that the Pharisees erred in their view of holiness. The Pharisees built their understanding and convictions on human traditions, which is a faulty foundation as we have seen. The most gifted teachers in their group spent many years deliberating and meditating to discover the most logical and reasonable means to achieve holiness, change, and growth. The end result of their labors was confusion, not clarification. This line of reasoning led to an endless string of regulations that governed nearly every dimension of life. The belief that exterior change can produce interior change

COPING AND LEGALISM: DEAD ENDS

became so accepted in Jesus' day that few even questioned it.

> Jesus called the crowd to him and said, "Listen and understand. What goes into a man's mouth does not make him 'unclean,' but what comes out of his mouth, that is what makes him 'unclean.'. . .
>
> "Are you still so dull?" Jesus asked them. "Don't you see that whatever enters the mouth goes into the stomach and then out of the body? But the things that come out of the mouth come from the heart, and these make a man 'unclean.' For out of the heart come evil thoughts, murder, adultery, sexual immorality, theft, false testimony, slander. These are what make a man 'unclean'; but eating with unwashed hands does not make him 'unclean.'"
>
> (Matthew 15:10–11, 16–20)

Paul deals with legalism in similar terms as Jesus. He first warns against allowing anyone to pressure us into conforming to an external practice through critical judging. He identifies issues relating to eating and drinking as two obvious matters subject to pressure. The Jews were easy victims due to their prior conditioning under the Old Testament dietary laws.

But the problem of legalism was not limited to Jewish Christians. The Gentile church soon established its own food regulations, and with the passing of time these regulations grew in complexity. Until recent years, for example, food restrictions were placed on Roman Catholics. It is not uncommon for Protestants to pat themselves on the back, thinking that they have avoided these obvious errors. After all, we never had to eat tuna salad on Fridays.

But wait! Paul says legalism is not limited to issues of food; it includes matters of drink as well. At this point many Protestants are equally vulnerable. Acceptable and unacceptable drinks have been hotly debated, particularly in the United States. What is the underlying reason for such debate? It is clearly the conviction that certain beverages will pollute you and drain away your holiness. Jesus spoke to this issue clearly by teaching that food and drink come into and then pass out of the body, never touching our holiness.

Paul continues his analysis of legalism by warning against judgmental attitudes arising from how we spend certain days. Specifically he warns against problems stemming from religious festivals, New Moon celebrations, and Sabbath regulations. The issue of when and how we spend religious holidays is answered by recognizing that it doesn't really make any difference. There are no New Testament guidelines in these areas. Christian liberty is the order of the day.

I find it interesting that Paul includes the Sabbath in this discussion. Quite clearly, the New Testament doesn't command the Sabbath principle upon the church. It ultimately wouldn't matter to God when we worship, any more than it matters where we worship (see

John 4). Such concerns are external. The real issue is how we worship, not in terms of ritual, but in terms of heart. The use of all days is God's concern and therefore all days are alike (Rom. 14:5, 6). Each day is to be lived surrendered to the lordship of Christ, not in alignment with external regulations.

In conclusion, Paul shows in verse 17 that all external regulations are but a shadow of things to come. The shadow points to the reality to be found in the person of Christ. We are not to spend our time in shadows, but walking in the light. A shadow has no reality apart from the object casting it. To see only the shadow leaves you guessing as to the specific appearance of the object casting it.

We are not called to be shadow-gazers, but Christ-gazers. We are to look upon Jesus, and the reality of freedom found in His grace. He is the mystery of God finally revealed, the object casting the shadow of Old Testament regulations.

To revert back to legalism is to live in the shadows. To believe external regulations will produce internal change is to be clouded to the truth.

◆ THREE ◆

"Secrets" and Self-Denial: Dead Ends

Do not let anyone who delights in false humility and the worship of angels disqualify you for the prize. Such a person goes into great detail about what he has seen, and his unspiritual mind puffs him up with idle notions. He has lost connection with the Head, from whom the whole body, supported and held together by its ligaments and sinews, grows as God causes it to grow.

(Colossians 2:18–19)

We have been examining the inadequate answers offered to those sincerely seeking change and growth in their lives, answers that present a dead end in the quest for holiness. Having examined the inadequacy of simply coping with life and the deceptions of legalism, we are now ready to turn attention to the next two dead ends Paul addresses in Colossians 2.

We will first examine the belief that the answer to change is found through discovering a "secret." Such a "secret" is discovered through experiencing mystical, spiritual experiences in which one gains a deeper knowledge of Christ than can be found through the objective facts in the written Word of God. Such a misunderstanding has led many into frustration and heartache.

This error in the Colossian church was the direct result of the influence of a heretical teaching called *Gnosticism*. Although a thorough examination of Gnosticism is beyond the purpose of this book, it is important to understand some of the implications of this heresy in relationship to the issue of change. Scholars agree that part of Paul's purpose in writing the epistle to the Colossian church was to refute Gnosticism. Let's briefly examine this philosophy and see how it approached the issue of change.

Gnosticism is a general title given to a variety of religious movements that existed at the time of the early development of the church. Although there were many variations in teaching, Gnostics were generally characterized by the following ideas:

First, Gnostics believed the material world in which we live was not the product of God, but rather the result of the work of a lesser, evil personage (demigod). As a result they believed that matter was inherently evil. Since we have physical bodies, these too were considered evil.

"SECRETS" AND SELF-DENIAL: DEAD ENDS

Second, Gnostics believed that salvation involved escaping from both our physical bodies and the material universe. They believed that such a salvation, although related to the work of Christ, was actually dependent upon gaining special insight, or secret knowledge. Such knowledge would result in allowing us to find such an escape. Since the Greek word for subjective, or experiential knowledge was *Gnosis*, the heresy came to be called Gnosticism.

Third, as a practical application of such beliefs, Gnostics viewed change as the outgrowth of gaining a mystical, secret knowledge from God, usually in the setting of a highly subjective, religious experience. Because such "secret" knowledge went beyond the Scriptures, the Scriptures became secondary in the search for truth and change.

Gnostic teaching had many important implications in the issues of incarnation, resurrection, and atonement. For our purposes, however, we will limit our examination to the implications related directly to change. Such implications have continued into our present day, surviving far longer than the heresy itself.[1]

The first implication of Gnosticism in the quest for change was the emphasis it placed on spiritual "guides." Since the knowledge one sought was a "secret," one must make a choice regarding who seems most likely to guide him to it. Such a choice rested upon the dual foundation of a person's claim to have found the "secret" and the attractiveness or persuasiveness of their life and speech. The result of all this was the search for the believer who seemed to have "arrived," a guru of sorts who promised the most likely pathway to "enlightenment."

Now it is both natural and proper for Christians to be drawn toward those who seem to have "arrived" in their Christian life. This is a healthy response when those attracting attention are clearly reflecting the fruit of the Spirit. We all should be attracted to the lifestyle of such people. Imitation is certainly a proper response in such cases. Notice Paul's attitude:

> *Whatever you have learned or received or heard from me, or seen in me—put it into practice.*
> (Philippians 4:9)

Unfortunately, people in Paul's day, as well as today, are also drawn toward those of questionable value, guides who lead them away from the Word of God and rest their hopes upon the subjective and mystical world of "secrets." The Gnostic and the contemporary possessor of "secrets" are cut from the same mold. God's answer to the foundational question of how to change will *never* be found in a "secret" known only to a few enlightened "guides." God's Word clearly reveals such an answer to *all* who seek it.

The second implication of Gnosticism in the quest for change was the belief that the answer for change went far beyond the Word of God

"SECRETS" AND SELF-DENIAL: DEAD ENDS

and rested upon secrets gained in visions, meditation, or prophecy. When facing such "secrets" it is crucial we remind ourselves of the promise in Colossians 2:2–3. All the understanding and insight that God is going to reveal is found in His Son Jesus Christ as the Scriptures have revealed Him. There are no other authoritative, or necessary, places to turn. The dead end of "secrets" is seen by this fact, that "secrets" encourage us to seek to find the pathway toward change through some means other than objective revelation in God's Word.

The third implication of Gnosticism in the quest for change is related to the very concept of spiritual maturity. The attraction of Gnosticism was often related to the personal charisma of its promoter, and so it is today with the issue of "secrets." Because of confusion regarding holiness and maturity, it's not uncommon to define maturity as being zealous for the Lord or having a deeply sensual love toward God. True spirituality, however, is reflected by faith, hope, and *agape* love, not the degree of "in-loveness" someone seems to feel toward God.

Some people are prone to be highly sensual in their relationship with God and therefore project an aura of spirituality impressive to Christians confused about true spirituality. Such a misunderstanding has often elevated certain people into a spiritual prominence not truly justified. The *proof* of spiritual truth is seen by its conformity to the written Word of God, not by the sincerity or sensuality of its proclaimer.

THE CHANGE FACTOR

The fourth implication of Gnosticism in the quest for change was a confusing of the purpose for seeking intimacy with God. As was already discussed, the religious "secrets" offered by the Gnostic inevitably went beyond the Scriptures. These "deeper truths" were claimed as the outgrowth of a sensual, mystical, and intimate relationship with God. In other words, intimacy with God is presented as the means of gaining true knowledge, or revelation, regarding our Christian life and practice. The essence of the error of Gnosticism and those who currently push "secrets" as a way of change, is seen in this very union between intimacy and revelation.

Church history has been filled with examples of this problem. From the "secrets" of the early Gnostics, to the "secrets" of medieval mystics such as Meister Eckhart and later to Madame Guyon and Fenelon, this problem has often led to heresy because of a growing disregard for God's Word in favor of mystical insight.[2]

How does all this relate to the issue of learning how to truly change? Simply in this way: we will never find change and growth in our lives through focusing on the answers offered through "secrets." God is a God of revelation, not concealment. He has not hidden the truth.

The fifth implication of Gnosticism in the quest for change related to the problem of spiritual elitism. Gnosticism promoted a type of spiritual class distinction. People were disqualified

"SECRETS" AND SELF-DENIAL: DEAD ENDS

from the enlightened spiritual class if their insight and practices didn't match up with the leader's "secrets." Such disqualification was part of Paul's concern in Colossians. In verse 18 the word "disqualify" means to deny a claim being made. Specifically, a claim to maturity would be denied on the basis of their "secrets." This resulted in the establishment of two classes of believers.

Such "divisions" were not limited to the early church. Even today the emphasis on "secrets" creates division in the church, a division that has far more to do with differences arising from feelings and subjective insights than differences in doctrine. "Secrets" cause divisions that reflect sensuality instead of spirituality.

Paul's intention was to help Christians escape the dead end of Gnosticism and "secrets." Now that we understand the five major implications of Gnosticism in the quest for change, let's examine how Paul reveals their error. He shows us several characteristics about Gnosticism and the emphasis on "secrets" that clearly show the inadequacy of the position for the Christian seeking God's answer for change.

The first characteristic is the stress "secrets" place on false humility. True humility is a Christian virtue and in Colossians 3:12 we find humility commended. Humility refers to a disposition of life in which one is able to keep the Creator and Creation distinctions clear. Such humility causes people to see themselves for what they really are and recognize the necessity of dependence on the Lord instead of becoming self-sufficient. That is the essence of the spiritual grace of humility.

False humility means gaining a penitential satisfaction from putting oneself down. Penance is defined as punishment undergone for the purpose of making amends for one's sin. The human tendency is to want to pay for all of our wrongs. Our natural inclination is to want to do penance before God. There is a penitential satisfaction gained from putting ourselves down. Paul speaks of such satisfaction when he says, "They delight in the false humility." Such an error can take different forms, physical, emotional, or spiritual. The Revised Standard Version translates the passage with the word "self-abasement" instead of "false humility." I feel this is closer to what is intended here. The emphasis is on putting ourselves down, hurting ourselves physically or emotionally through fasting, painful practices, and self-denial for the dual purpose of trying to pay for sin and grow out of our weaknesses. Those who accept this emphasis inevitably fall into the ironic trap of taking great pride in their humility.

The second characteristic of Gnosticism and the contemporary emphasis on "secrets" that reveal their inherent inadequacy is their tendency to take stands on visions and not the Word. Although this was previously noted, let's examine it in more detail. The RSV translates verse

"SECRETS" AND SELF-DENIAL: DEAD ENDS

18 as "taking a stand," in contrast to the NIV translation of "great details." The RSV is a little plainer at this point. The Greek literally means going into great detail, but the context shows the reason for going into great detail is to justify why they do what they do and why they believe what they believe. They take their stands not on the Word, but on visions. Visions are notorious for being misleading.

Visions should not be sought and certainly are not a means of finding change in our lives. Visions can come from all kinds of sources, including the pizza you ate late last night. Frequently visions have led Christians into beliefs and practices that are actually in conflict with the Word. For example, this passage refers to those who, taking stands on visions, challenge people to worship angels. The Gnostics believed that their "secrets" were gained through angelic teachers, not directly from God Himself. They taught that such angels (or beings) can intercede for us with God and should thus be venerated.

The applications of such "venerated intercessors" to such issues as the veneration of Mary and saints should be obvious. Such Gnostic veneration was based upon subjective visions, not the Word of God. To confront a Gnostic by claiming that the Word of God doesn't teach us to worship angels, would be futile. Such individuals would simply answer, "But God showed me that this is what we are suppose to do. He showed it to me in a vision." Such an answer closes the discussion because they would believe none could argue with their experience.

We might look at such a problem and feel that such a Gnostic emphasis would never convince us of their position. Yet before we begin to feel too smug and secure, let's remember that church history is full of examples where, long after Gnosticism was dead and gone, visions led people into all sorts of abuses and errors that the Word of God never supported and that they themselves never believed would be possible. Even today the authority of visions remains a real issue of concern within the various segments of Christianity. Paul's arguments are truly timely.

We need to recognize that God is never going to reveal something through a vision that is absolutely necessary for someone to change and grow. God has already said that the full understanding of this process is found in Christ and in the Word. Visions will never be an additional source of revelation and therefore authoritative. The Holy Spirit is the author of revelation and has, in these last days, concluded that work within the limits of the written Word of God. The ministry of the Holy Spirit that we should seek is illumination, or insight into the written Word. The Holy Spirit is never going to guide us into "secrets."

Such a search for "secrets," or additional revelation from God, inevitably produces a problem of pride in one's life. To feel we have

"SECRETS" AND SELF-DENIAL: DEAD ENDS

"found" something hidden from others tends to puff us up. In fact, Paul identifies the Gnostics as "puffed-up" ones.

Those into "secrets" tend to pride themselves on the insights that they have and their ability to teach them in detail. There seems no end of words to their position as they elaborate on all the extrabiblical insight that God has blessed them with. The answers they offer are based on human pride and reason, not God's revelation. Thus they fall under the discussion of the previous chapter on coping.

Gnosticism and "secrets" are a dead end. Their true deadness is demonstrated in verse 19: "He has lost connection with the Head...." The fact is, someone is not growing at all when he has fallen into these traps. They've lost connection with the source of growth who is Christ. All growth proceeds from Christ. It is only as we are looking to Christ that we grow. These people have lost connection with Him.

SELF-DENIAL

There is one more dead end remaining to be examined, and we find it in verses 20–23. The issue is the dead end of self-denial.

> Since you died with Christ to the basic principles of this world, why, as though you still belonged to it, do you submit to its rules: "Do not handle! Do not taste! Do not touch!"? These are all destined to perish with use, because they are based on human commands and teachings. Such

THE CHANGE FACTOR

> regulations indeed have an appearance of wisdom, with their self-imposed worship, their false humility and their harsh treatment of the body, but they lack any value in restraining sensual indulgence.
>
> (Colossians 2:20–23)

The error of self-denial as the means to change and growth is closely related to the problem of legalism examined in the previous chapter. Although related, this error is distinctive enough to merit its own treatment. The key error or deception is to equate self-denial with spiritual commitment and maturity.

The deception here is very subtle. The error arises when we think that self-denial will cause us to become mature or maintain our maturity, or when we come to the point of believing that self-denial is maturity. On the basis of such an error, many unsaved, but highly disciplined people would have to be seen as spiritual. We can easily slip into this subtle error. Self-denial is also, unfortunately, a devastating error because it leads us to a lifetime of self-effort instead of surrender, drawing on our own resources instead of Christ's power.

Self-denial takes the form of a stress on self-imposed disciplines. The error manifests itself in a clear way in much of the current emphasis on discipleship. Often those teaching on discipleship will tell a person that the pathway to true discipleship rests upon the development of a certain set of habits of life. Discipleship becomes

"SECRETS" AND SELF-DENIAL: DEAD ENDS

defined as little more than the process of developing self-disciplines. I've been guilty of this error at times in my own teaching. Part of my growing disillusionment with much that is said about becoming a disciple is that ultimately the task has been corrupted into little more than a stress on self-disciplines. Growth means gritting your teeth long enough to allow spiritual habits to become part of your life.

This error is also encountered in other areas. In the area of dieting, for example, teachings often imply that if through self-denial we can become self-disciplined in our eating, we will somehow become a better Christian. The promise given ties becoming a more mature Christian with becoming more disciplined in your eating. The error is also seen in the area of devotions. The promise here implies that consistency in your devotions would equal maturity. We lose sight of the fact that it is not the self-discipline, but rather the Word that makes you grow. This is a subtle shift, yet an important one.
Self-denial can be found lurking within many areas of Christian teaching.

The principle behind this error can be summarized in this way: Self-denial and self-effort in any area of your life will translate or transfer into growth in other areas. The principle promises that God will reward our self-efforts and self-denials with maturity and spiritual growth. Sometimes the principle is very plainly stated, other times it is more subtle. Yet whatever the form, the false promise is there that if we only become more disciplined people, God will reward such discipline by granting us change that is real and bring us into maturity.

> *Are you so foolish? After beginning with the spirit, are you now trying to attain your goal by human effort?*
>
> (Galatians 3:3)

In this verse we find God's response to this error. Any "change" that comes from self-effort and self-denial is a self-imposed change, external not internal, not Spirit-produced. Any such "change" is dependent on our continued strength and discipline in order to maintain it. Why? Because we have never really changed. We've just added some new patterns of life, some new habits that are dependent upon our self-effort to maintain. Only the Spirit of God can change people inside.

There are several other insights in Colossians into the error of self-denial. First, Paul says our efforts will perish with use. That means that they don't stand the test of time. We give them up because either we can't seem to achieve the discipline we want, or if we do gain the discipline, we realize over time that we really haven't changed inside. Over time, self-imposed habits prove themselves to be invalid as far as producing true maturity, true Christlikeness, in our hearts. The promise proves empty and perishes with time. We will always be disappointed

"SECRETS" AND SELF-DENIAL: DEAD ENDS

when we look to a particular habit to produce Christlikeness in us. Its benefit will be purely external, if it benefits us at all. There will be no internal change.

Second, in verse 22 Paul shows that the truth about self-denial is that the teaching is based on man's ideas, not God's. Human commands and teachings can have the appearance of wisdom, but not the reality of truth. Human logic often increases the deception because self-denial and self-effort seems so reasonable and logical a way to change. Self-effort is logical and reasonable, but it is false. What it builds is self-righteousness, not holiness, and religious pride in those who depend on it.

Different people have different natural abilities when it comes to developing self-imposed disciplines in their lives. For some self-discipline is not too difficult and there are few areas of their life where they couldn't grit their teeth and achieve a degree of external conformity to a certain goal or standard. Others will fall flat on their faces in almost any area they work at. As a result, people with a high degree of self-determination will often fall into the trap of pride over their accomplishments.

The real variable in the successful development of self-imposed disciplines is personality, not maturity. Some people can be more self-disciplined than others. I believe in many cases such an ability becomes a detriment rather than a help in true growth in Christ because it keeps us from being fully surrendered. It keeps us from being clearly aware of our own inadequacies so that we become dependent on the Lord.

Third, in verse 23 Paul shows the emphasis on self-effort and self-denial inevitably leads to self-imposed worship, worship on our terms and in our strength. We fall into this trap when we try to worship God on the basis of external actions instead of the heart. Such an approach leads to rules and regulations. Notice God's view in Isaiah 29:13:

> "These people come near to me with their mouth and honor me with their lips, but their hearts are far from me. Their worship of me is made up only of rules taught by men.

This is the same concept in Colossians, where Paul warns against worship that becomes a concept of regulation and not the heart. Worship is a heart issue, a relationship issue. Those whom the Father wishes to have worship Him are those who worship in spirit and in truth. Worship has nothing to do with whether we meet in a gym or in a sanctuary, whether we sing a certain type of music, whether the service lasts one hour or three hours, or whether we meet on Friday night or Sunday morning. Worship is an issue of the heart of the people. The emphasis on self-denial encourages us to focus on the externals and the regulations in our worship of God.

"SECRETS" AND SELF-DENIAL: DEAD ENDS

The King James Version uses the phrase "will worship." That's the concept. It's worship growing out of the will—"I will to worship"—instead of our hearts naturally responding to God because of the life of Christ in us and the Spirit of God's presence.

Fourth, Paul shows that the emphasis on externals and self-denial will promote harsh treatment of the body. This inevitably occurs because of the pervasive belief that the body itself is sinful and it needs harsh treatment. Such a view of the body is false and unbiblical and has stuck around far longer than the Gnostic proponents who formulated the position. The body was created by God and is good. Due to the fall of Adam our physical body deteriorates and is susceptible to sin. Because of such weakness (not sinfulness), our body needs assistance, not abasement.

The issue is to whom will we surrender our body. If we surrender to sin, the outcome is going to be negative. Such an outcome is not because the body is bad, but rather because it is weak and sin can take control of our physical members. But when we surrender our bodies to Christ and allow Christ to live through us, the outcome is going to be positive. We will discover our body is able to align with God's creative purposes. Such surrender is the real answer to keeping sin under control in our physical body.

Remember, rooted deeply in the error of self-denial is the concept that there is something inherently wrong with the body. That is not a biblical teaching. We don't need to punish our bodies. The atonement was already made. We don't need to treat ourselves harshly, to somehow do penance for sin, or to somehow keep our bodies from breaking into sin.

We have already seen that sin is not a question of the external working in, but rather the internal working out. We can subject our physical bodies to forms of self-denial for the rest of our lives and that will not protect us from breaking out into sin, because it is inside that the decision is made. The internal then works out through the members. It is out of the heart that we fall. We don't need to treat our bodies harshly and practice self-denial in the hope that such action will somehow check sin.

Finally, the ultimate putdown of the passage is shown in the last phrase of verse 23. Here we discover the ultimate demonstration of the inherent weakness of self-denial, that is, it is of no value in restraining sensual indulgence. What is sensual indulgence? It is giving in to sin-aroused passions in our life. Self-denial doesn't really solve the sin problem. Self-denial does not change the part of us that we want to change.

Physical training is of some value....
(1 Timothy 4:8)

"SECRETS" AND SELF-DENIAL: DEAD ENDS

The Scriptures show we can find some value in physical training. Its value is found in our physical well-being. The deception uncovered in this passage in Colossians is the belief that physical training results in spiritual growth. This error motivates us to be training ourselves physically because we think it will result in spirituality. The value of self-denial and the development of disciplined habits is purely an external value. Such a fact doesn't make the development of godly habits unimportant, but we must recognize that the value will not be the spiritual change that transforms us in the inner man.

It is only when we realize our inherent weakness and begin to look to Christ for strength beyond our own that growth can occur. We don't have sufficient resources in ourselves to achieve true personal transformation. We might find sufficient resources in ourselves to train our bodies and develop certain habits of life, but we will never find sufficient resources to change our hearts. Remember Jeremiah 17:9? The heart is beyond human cure. Only Christ can change our heart. In order to truly change, we must focus on what it means to know Christ and allow Him to minister to us. To focus on these dead ends will never lead to change in our lives.

To this point we have been focused on the negative, that is, detecting erroneous arguments or answers as to how to find real change in one's life. Let's briefly recap these false answers, these dead ends, before turning to the true answer presented in God's Word.

Paul first warns against settling for coping instead of changing. The world has no way to actually change someone's heart and, as a result, focuses its attention on learning to cope more effectively with ourselves and our weaknesses. Such a focus has resulted in a degree of help for many who simply are unable to cope with life. As commendable as this outcome is, the solution always falls far short of God's intentions. God is interested in transforming us, not simply enabling us to cope with our personality. All such solutions based on coping are characterized by dependence upon man's efforts instead of the Lord's.

Paul next warns against the futility of legalism as a means to change. Legalism is defined here as the concept that change begins on the outside and progresses to the inner man. Holiness is understood as first external and later internal. The solution offered always involves aligning with various regulations governing behavior, with the promise of eventual inner change growing out of such activity. The inadequacy of this answer was clearly explained by Christ's teachings in the Gospels regarding the true direction for change, that is, inside to outside and not the reverse.

The apostle's third warning had to do with the dead end of seeking after religious "secrets." Such an emphasis will lead us into becoming

"SECRETS" AND SELF-DENIAL: DEAD ENDS

dependent upon subjective religious experiences as the means to change, instead of the objective Word of God. The search for religious "secrets" as the way to become a truly changed person, will never lead to change, but rather lead into many heartaches, deceptions, and loss of connection with the Head, from Whom true change is achieved.

Paul's fourth dead end was self-denial. Essentially this deception was the belief that self-effort and the development of discipline habits of living would produce change in the inner man. Many people who strive to live a more disciplined life end up trusting in those self-imposed disciplines to produce holiness and change. They believe that self-effort in one aspect of their life will carry over to other areas of their life, ultimately affecting their spiritual condition.

Scripture plainly shows the dead end in this teaching. Self-effort is exactly that, "self" effort. Self-reliance will never produce spiritual change within our hearts. As we grow in the Lord and are truly changed, part of the fruit of that will be growing discipline in life. But such discipline is the outcome, not the means toward achieving, the change in the inner man. God is certainly interested in seeing people disciplined and living productive lives but these goals are meant to be the outcome of inner change. They are not the things that produce the change in our life.

We are now ready to turn attention to the

positive. Now that we know how *not* to grow and change, how do we in fact discover the change we so desperately seek? It is the answer to this question to which Paul now turns his attention.

NOTES

1. For further study on Gnosticism, see the following:

J. D. Douglas, ed., *The New International Dictionary of the Christian Church* (Grand Rapids: Zondervan, 1974), 416–17.

Earle E. Cairns, *Christianity Through the Centuries* (Grand Rapids: Zondervan, 1967), 105–7.

2. See the following for more understanding of mysticism in church history:

Cairns, *Christianity Through the Centuries*, 108–9, 271–75.

Douglas, *The New International Dictionary of the Christian Church*, 691–92.

◆ FOUR ◆

God's Formula For Change

For though I am absent from you in body, I am present with you in spirit and delight to see how orderly you are and how firm your faith in Christ is. So then, just as you received Christ Jesus as Lord, continue to live in him, rooted and built up in him, strengthened in the faith as you were taught, and overflowing with thankfulness.

(Colossians 2:5–7)

Now that we have examined the ways change will never occur, we can turn attention to the true answers for our quest. God definitely has an answer, a plan, He intends to follow in bringing each of us into conformity with His Son Jesus Christ.

THE CHANGE FACTOR

In chapter 1, the word "change" was defined as the progressive transformation of a person's characteristic ways of thinking, feeling, and acting. Change is a *process* in which God gradually conforms our personality into the image of Jesus Christ. In other words, change is the gradual infiltration into our mind, emotions, and behavior of the new creation we became at salvation. As Christians we will only discover this process of change taking place when we respond in obedience to the specific (and only) plan God has ordained for such personal transformation. The key factor in God's plan can be summarized by the phrase *"Faith in Christ."* Let's now examine these verses in Colossians to understand just how faith in Christ is meant to apply practically to our goal of personal change.

The role that faith in Christ plays in the process of change first becomes clear in verse 5. In this verse Paul shows that the firmness of the Colossians' faith in Christ was the primary reason for his optimism and confidence about their spiritual lives. The word translated "firm" connotes two ideas in the Greek, namely, persistence and centrality. Thus "firm" first refers to the *persistence* of faith in Christ in the Colossian church. They had continued to hold fast to the truths of the Gospel in the face of many trials and heresies. Paul previously stressed the need for such persistence in chapter 1, verse 23.

GOD'S FORMULA FOR CHANGE

> ... continue in your faith, established and firm, not moved from the hope held out in the gospel.

"Firm" secondly refers to the *centrality* of faith in Christ to the daily lives of the Colossian believers. Somehow the Colossians had discovered that faith in Christ had great applicability, not only to their salvation, but to their unfolding Christian experience as well. In God's plan, Christ is pertinent to our daily lives, not simply our eternal destinies. To understand this pertinence, we must go on to verse 6.

GOD'S FORMULA

Paul turns attention in verse 6 to the practical benefits of a persisting, firm faith in Christ. He shows that there is a definite continuity between our first act of faith in Christ at salvation and our continuing faith in Christ in daily living. In so doing, Paul elaborates on the basic formula for change in the Christian life. The formula can be summarized in the following way:

WE LIVE THE SAME WAY WE RECEIVED

Paul is teaching us that there is a clear connection, or continuity, between the actions and attitudes we had when we first received Christ and the attitudes and actions we are to have in our daily Christian experience. We are to *live* (or *walk*, as some translations put it) in the same fashion we *received* Christ. In other words, transformation of our personality into the image of Christ is going to occur in the same general way that new birth and salvation were achieved.

THE CHANGE FACTOR

Think for a moment about when you received Jesus Christ as Savior and Lord. What was the critical response in your life that resulted in salvation? Clearly it was the act of placing your *faith* in Christ. Therefore, Paul shows us that the concept connecting our walking and receiving is the issue of *faith*. Faith in Christ is pertinent to salvation *and* sanctification!

Verse 6 is a command, something God requires us to choose to do. Walking (or living) as we received is an issue of obedience in our Christian life. To obey this command we must first understand what faith means. Thus the key question is how does one actually live as he received, or better, how does one live by the faith he expressed when he first received Christ? To adequately answer this crucial question we must first define what the Bible means by the term *faith* and how such faith can be focused upon the issues we face in day-to-day living.

THE MEANING OF FAITH

Understanding the biblical definition of faith is critical to our Christian living, and I previously explored this issue in the book *The Dynamics of Faithful Living*.[1] I wish to quote a section that specifically defines the word faith and enables us to understand its use in the Book of Colossians.

GOD'S FORMULA FOR CHANGE

> ... Living by faith in the Old Testament meant having a life characterized by firm certainty and trust, demonstrated clearly by obedience, while all the while sensing a healthy awe for the God who is there.
>
> In the New Testament there is even more expansion given on the content of the word faith. The word most often translated faith in the New Testament comes from various forms of the Greek word pistis. Pistis, as a secular word, meant to rely on something, to believe or trust in something, to accept something as being true and as a result to commit yourself to something. All of these connotations were part of the secular uses of this word. Although used in a variety of settings, the basic idea, in the case of a person or thing, was responding to that person or thing on the basis of a confidence, a reliance, an acceptance and a commitment. All of these ideas roll around together in the meaning of the word.

I believe it to be very significant that the Greek word *pistis* was never used in religious ways until just about the time the New Testament was written. Thus faith was not initially a religious word, and had no religious overtones or connotations. The New Testament writers, under the inspiration of the Spirit, took a word that was initially a secular word and applied it in relationship to God. This added additional perspective to our knowledge of what a life of faith was all about. It is difficult for us today to grasp the impact of the word *pistis* in the New

Testament culture. To be as free of the often ambiguous connotations the word "faith" has gained in our culture due to its nearly exclusive use in religious contexts would be a blessing. Such a benefit was graciously bestowed upon the early church.

The word "faith" was always used with an object in the Greek. Faith demanded, and was meaningless apart from, an object. Thus we recognize very quickly that in the Scriptures the word faith is not at all like the word that is used often today in reference to some sort of detached feeling inside of a person. Faith is a response to an object. For the Christian it is a response to God and what He reveals about Himself. We need to understand clearly that biblical faith is always an objective word, always focused on God and His Word. It is not just a feeling. Often people think it really doesn't matter what you have faith in, just as long as you have faith. Such a perspective is foreign to the Scripture's use of the word. The object of one's faith is crucial.[2]

In summary, faith is an act of trust and commitment focused on God and what He promises. It is a very personal and objective word. How then does this understanding of faith relate to the formula for change presented by Paul in verse 6? First of all, this definition shows that when we became Christians our faith was demonstrated by receiving Christ's atoning work at Calvary, *accepting Christ* to be our personal Savior and *committing* ourselves to follow Him as our Lord. Such a faith response mandated that we turn from our self-reliance and begin total dependence upon Christ (true concept behind repentance) for acceptance with God. This is the first part of the formula, namely, the receiving.

Second, this definition shows what it means to live, or walk, by faith. Specifically, faith (trust in Christ and what He promises) shows itself by turning from our self-reliance and being Christ-dependent for our growth and personality transformation. There is clearly a common thread of faith that runs throughout our Christian life. It starts with salvation and continues on from that beginning. Faith in Christ is the connecting link that provides the common denominator of Christian living. This should not come as a surprise to us, as Paul previously identified Christ in 1:18 as the one who is preeminent, or supreme, in *all* things (including Christian growth).

It is Christ who is *always* meant to be at the center of our hopes, whether for eternal life or personal transformation. Such trust, acceptance and commitment to Christ is God's formula for change. Saving faith and sanctifying faith are thus cut from the same mold. Our faith is always centered on Christ, but differs in regard to the specific work we are trusting Him to do.

In Colossians Paul is amplifying this concept of faith living. What does God really desire from us? The answer is faith in Christ, whether the issue is salvation or growth. It is not what we are able to do personally, but rather what we trust Christ to do in us that produces growth. We are to live by faith because we received Christ by faith. Just as we trusted in Christ's work on our behalf in salvation, so we are to trust Christ's work *within* us to provide both enablement and personality transformation. We were saved by trusting Christ's work and we are sanctified by trusting Christ's work. God's formula for change definitely shows faith's continuity for our lives. Let's examine this crucial concept in more depth.

God intends our response to Him to be the same throughout our Christian life. As Paul puts it in Hebrews:

> *And without* faith *it is impossible to please God.* . . .
>
> (Hebrews 11:6)

At the beginning we are to place our faith in Christ's work upon the cross. Although the work of Christ upon the cross will always be the center and foundation of our confidence for right standing with God, God also intends us to have faith in the ongoing ministry of Christ within the life of each believer. Faith finds its first expression when we determine to turn from our own works, our self-reliance, and trust in what Christ has done for us on the cross.

Our faith finds its continuing expression when we turn from self-reliance and trust in the work Christ is doing within and through us. Such trust is not synonymous with passivity however, as we shall discover in later chapters. For now it must suffice to show faith's continuity in God's formula for change.

We are to trust Christ to do within us what is impossible for us to achieve on our own. Specifically this involves three things, i.e. heart change, victory over sin, and fruit in ministry. As a daily choice we determine to place our reliance upon the indwelling Christ to control our lives. Throughout the day we also choose to live in a Christ-dependent manner whenever the tendency toward self-sufficiency rears its head.

Paul, in verse 7, now shows what living by God's formula produced in the past and what it will produce in the present. He does this by examining three phrases that demonstrate the effect faith in Christ has in growth and change. In essence, Paul provides a rationale for such a step of faith in the Christian's life.

FACTORS IN THE FORMULA

Factor 1: Faith gave us union with Christ (when we received). First we need to realize that we are rooted in Christ through our faith. "Rooted" is a perfect participle which indicates a past action with continuing benefits. It is also in the passive voice showing the action is done to us, not by us. It refers to what happened in the past in response to our faith that has continuing benefits for us. Beyond the obvious answer of salvation, Paul is referring to the truth that we were placed in union with Christ when we first believed. Theologically this is referred to as our mystical union with Christ. This doctrine has important implications for our lives. Simply stated, our faith has brought us into a new relationship with Christ where we are intimately connected to His life. Biblically it now is accurate to say we are *in* Christ and He is *in* us. We remain distinct, yet are united in a deeply spiritual way. This union was the result of the baptizing ministry of God's Holy Spirit.

The Bible uses several analogies to enable us to comprehend *some* of what union is all about. We discover our union with Christ is like a vine and branches (John 15), a foundation and building (1 Peter 2), and a head and body (Ephesians 4). Our faith not only gave us new birth, but also changed our relationship to God. Christ is not only with us, but lives *in* us. This is Paul's point in Galatians 2:20.

> *I have been crucified with Christ and I no longer live, but Christ lives in me. The life I live in the body, I live by faith in the Son of God, who loved me and gave himself for me.*

So what are the implications of this "rooting"? The first is *assurance* of our salvation. We are already rooted, it is not a present command. We can't focus properly on the issue of change if we aren't certain we are His and that He lives within us already. Do you know you are rooted

GOD'S FORMULA FOR CHANGE

deeply into Christ and now are a part of His body? Our faith in Christ rooted us in Christ when we responded to the Gospel. We know this because God's Word promises it.

The second implication of "rooting" is *confidence*. If we are in union with Christ then He lives within us. If Christ lives within us then He can make a difference in our daily lives. In understanding union with Christ we gain the needed confidence to trust in His enablement to grow and change. As Paul puts it in 1:27, "Christ *in* you, the hope of glory."

Factor 2: Living faith enables us to grow (as we live). The second element of living by faith is the idea of growth. We were *rooted* in Christ so that we could *grow* in Him. Growth is God's clear intention for each of our lives. Yet our growth is dependent upon Christ's work within us. "Built up" is a present participle, which shows the action is an ongoing activity. It is in the passive voice, thus showing the action is done to us, not by us. Being built up in Christ is ultimately God's responsibility, but it rests upon the variable of our faith.

The construction of this passage is very interesting. We are commanded to live by faith so we can be built up in Christ. In the Greek the idea is that the growth is held together by Christ, or is dependent upon His action and presence. This is similar to the idea in Colossians 1:16–17 where we discover all things hold together in Christ. He is intended by the Father to be the center of everything, including our growth. Not only is growth dependent upon Christ, but it is also *maintained* by Christ. Personal growth remains *only* when Christ remains central in our lives. It is not a permanent possession. In other words, our personality will go back to reflecting our old nature if we stop living in Christ dependency. Faith *must* persist throughout our lives.

So what are the applications of being built up in Christ? The first is to see that apart from Christ we can do nothing. He is the source of our salvation *and* our growth. We can only be built up in Him, not in ourselves. There is no other option open to us to discover change.

The second application is to recognize we can never outgrow our dependence on Christ. We are to *live* by faith in Christ, not simply *begin* by faith in Christ. Any growth will always be in Him. God intends Christ to be central and indispensable to our Christian life. He doesn't gradually wean us away from such Christ dependency. I will never be able to be self-sufficient and adequate in my Christian walk. Christ will always need to be the center focus of my life. The end will be as it was in the beginning. Growth is maintained *only* by Christ.

The third application is that our life of dependency on Christ will produce a life that reflects Christ. In other words, Christ-dependency breeds Christlikeness in our lives. This is the promise of Galatians 5:22–23. The fruit of the

Spirit is the fruit of Christlikeness. This fruit is increasingly reflected in our personalities as we live a life of Christ dependency. The reason for this fruit will be explained as we turn attention to the remainder of the Colossians passage. Notice Paul's goal in Galatians 4:19:

> My dear children, for whom I am again in the pains of childbirth until Christ is formed in you. . . .

Factor 3: We appropriate strength only by faith (as we live). The third rationale of living by faith has to do with how we appropriate the power to grow and change in our Christian lives. Paul tells us that we discover strength as we place our faith in Christ. In other words, faith is the instrument of appropriation. The Greek construction here is quite difficult and has resulted in several possible renderings of verse 7. I feel the best translation would be this:

> . . . strengthened through your faith, even as you have always been taught.

The phrase "in the faith" is a dative in the instrumental case (Lightfoot) which shows that faith is the means through which one is strengthened, not the thing to be strengthened. The phrase "as you were taught" means even as, or according to. Thus the idea is that strength through faith is not a new idea, but rather an essential and consistent part of the apostle's teaching.

"Strengthened" is a present participle in the passive voice, showing the action is done to us, not by us. In other words, strength for Christian growth and living is *not* something we will produce on our own. Instead it is something given to us by another. Of course the source is shown to be Christ Himself.

It is at just this point that so many Christians get confused. It is not enough to know *what* God desires to see happen in our lives, we must also know *how* God intends to accomplish His desires. If we attempt to align with God's Word in our own strength, we will inevitably find failure and frustration in the process. We will *always* find ourselves ultimately inadequate because God intends to provide power for growth and obedience from outside of ourselves. It is Christ who provides the power for living this life, as Paul so clearly puts it in Philippians 4:13.

> *I can do everything through him who gives me strength.*

The word translated "strengthened" in Colossians 2:7 is *bebaioo*, which means to make stable, firm, secure, and established. The concept is basically that God works within us to establish our lives in victory as we place our faith in Christ. The root of our confidence and assurance about growth rests in the certainty of God's work within us. Our security for success stems from our faith in Christ which is demonstrated

GOD'S FORMULA FOR CHANGE

by a consistent turning away from self-confidence and resting entirely upon His power within us. His strength shows itself in our lives by the enablement to defeat sin's temptation and the transforming of our personalities.

As I already pointed out, Paul is not challenging us to have a stronger faith. Instead, we are promised a personal experience of strength from Christ when we place our faith in Him. Such a promise had always been the focus of Paul's teachings. "As you were taught" refers to this idea of Paul's consistency in message. Teaching is an important variable in growing in Christ, yet the focus of these verses is upon the *consistency* of the message, not its *necessity*.

In summary, this third rationale for living by faith applies to our lives by challenging us to recognize that God never intended us to be able to live the Christian life on our own power. We are to seek a strength beyond our own, a strength found *only* in Christ. We appropriate this strength as we *trust* in Christ to live through us. This act of *faith* is the means of discovering the power to face life and grow as Christians.

This is the crucial concept. Only God can bring about change in the heart of a man. Only when Christ is living through an individual will the changed heart begin to be reflected in a transforming personality. Such an individual's life will demonstrate to the world far more than simply an ethical system. We can admire an ethical system and certainly would rather be around someone who is ethical than someone who is not, but there is a difference in an individual's life when there is an alive Christ or a dead system. A very distinctive difference. We are called upon to communicate to the world the life of Jesus Christ living through us and in us.

In the final phrase in verse 7, Paul turns attention to our response to these truths. Basically our response has to do with giving credit where credit is due. In other words, a life of faith must be accompanied by a lifestyle of thanksgiving. Paul says a Christian should be overflowing with thanksgiving. This is a very frequent challenge in God's Word. Consider the following verses, for example:

> *Give thanks in all circumstances, for this is God's will for you in Christ Jesus.*
> (1 Thessalonians 5:18)
>
> *Always giving thanks to God the Father for everything, in the name of our Lord Jesus Christ.*
> (Ephesians 5:20)

It is interesting to notice that this last phrase is a present participle in the active voice. This shows it is we who are responsible for carrying it out. In the rest of the verse the focus is on divine activity.

I believe there are two major reasons for Paul's emphasis on thanksgiving. First, a lifestyle of giving thanks to God allows us to be re-

GOD'S FORMULA FOR CHANGE

minded of God's hand in everything in our lives. Such acknowledgment prevents the problem of forgetting God's role in our life. Constant reminders are necessary for a naturally forgetful creature like man. As we acknowledge God's hand we are led to continued surrender to His power and purpose. Secondly, thanksgiving prevents our tendency toward self-sufficiency. We are prone to believe we can handle life on our own. We are apt to think we were responsible for whatever has happened in the past. Thanksgiving breaks such deception within us. God warns against our tendency toward self-sufficiency.

> *You may say to yourself, "My power and the strength of my hands have produced this wealth for me." But remember the LORD your God, for it is he who gives you the ability to produce....*
> (Deuteronomy 8:17–18)
>
> *"I am the vine; you are the branches. If a man remains in me and I in him, he will bear much fruit; apart from me you can do nothing."*
> (John 15:5)

Thanksgiving assists us in keeping a correct view of ourselves and an honoring view of the Lord. It isn't merely playing a word game. When we meditate upon the issues for which we give God thanks, our own finiteness comes into clearer focus. Giving thanks in all circumstances is a clear demonstration of true Christ-dependency.

The foundation is now laid. We grow and change through a lifestyle of faith. We trust Christ for growth and change in the same way we trusted Him for salvation. Such a life of faith will flow from being rooted in Christ and will develop us into His image and be accomplished through His power. Thanksgiving is the key to keeping these truths in perspective.

NOTES

1. Gary W. Kuhne, *The Dynamics of Faithful Living* (Grand Rapids: Zondervan, 1983).

2. Ibid., 5ff.

◀ FIVE ▶

Faith and Fullness

We've been studying the issue of personality transformation and how to initiate change in the Christian life. We have seen that there are many answers given to explain the mechanics of such change, but most are of little help, and many are actually deceptions. We next examined God's formula for change. We discovered that Paul presents in Colossians 2:6–7 the truth that faith in Christ is at the core of real growth and change. The formula summarizes by saying we *live* as we *received*. In other words, faith in Christ is as important to Christian growth as it was to salvation. In the same way we received Christ Jesus we are to continue to live in Him.

Such a formula for growth, namely, faith in

THE CHANGE FACTOR

Christ, is reasonable because of three important ministries that occur in response to such faith. First, faith is the reason we were rooted in (or in union with) Christ. Second, God has determined that only faith enables us to benefit from His work of building us. Third, strength is appropriated only through our faith in Christ. Faith in Christ is most definitely the change factor in Christian living.

Faith is intended to be the thread, or continuity, of our lives. The thread begins when we trust in what Christ has accomplished for us upon the cross. We rest in the forgiveness and reconciliation with God made possible by Christ's sacrifice. The thread continues to weave through our lives as we choose to trust Christ for the enablement to face the needs of daily living.

We are now ready to continue our examination of why the formula works, or why faith in Christ can reasonably be expected to produce personality transformation. What other reasons does Paul present to explain why trusting in Christ to live in us and through us is the key to our growth and transformation in our personality? The answer to these questions is found in the following verses.

> *For in Christ all the fullness of the Deity lives in bodily form, and you have been given fullness in Christ, who is the head over every power and authority.*
>
> (Colossians 2:9–10)

FAITH AND FULLNESS

In these verses we encounter two additional reasons why consistently living as we received—that is, by faith in Christ—really works to produce a progressive transformation of our personalities. First, such faith in Christ works because of who Jesus Christ is. Second, such faith in Christ works because of what Jesus Christ has done within the life of a believer to give him fullness. Let's begin by examining the first reason—who Jesus Christ really is.

These verses begin by asserting that all the fullness of God dwelt in Jesus Christ. Paul is turning attention to the doctrine of the Trinity, a doctrine with implications for growth as well as salvation. He is affirming that Jesus Christ is truly the Second Person of the triune God. Now such an affirmation of deity is meant to be more than an abstract theological concept. This truth is intended to have practical implications for our faith. The Scriptures affirm the deity of Christ in many places, for example:

> *In the beginning was the Word, and the Word was with God, and the Word was God. . . . The Word became flesh and made his dwelling among us.*
>
> (John 1:1, 14)
>
> *He is the image of the invisible God, the firstborn over all creation. For by him all things were created: . . . all things were created by him and for him. He is before all things, and in him all things hold together.*
>
> (Colossians 1:15–17)

Jesus Christ is actually and truly God. This truth makes all the difference in the world in the practical consideration of finding growth and change. If Jesus were merely a man, even a perfect man, what He did could make no difference for us today in terms of change in our lives. The benefit we would gain would be limited to simply having an example to follow. Only God has the capability of omnipresence, which allows Him to be everywhere and minister in everyone. Being truly God, Jesus Christ had that possibility and potential. Because He is God He can dwell in each one of us in a very personal way. Only God is omnipotent, all-powerful, and has the ability to do what we cannot do on our own. Because He is God and has all the power of divine nature dwelling in Him, Christ can and will produce real change in each one of us.

Our view of Christ can have significant implications in our understanding of Christian living. Obviously, if we don't recognize His deity, we will see Christ as only an example for us to imitate. Yet, even if we accept Christ's deity it is possible to overlook its implications. We can particularly overlook the reality of His indwelling presence and enabling power.

A good diagnostic test would be to evaluate our daily Christian experience. If Christ were somehow unable to continue His indwelling and enablement would it make that great a difference? For many Christians the answer would have to be no. They are living the Christian life depending on their own strength and abilities instead of relying on Christ. As you remember, a key weakness of the various dead ends to change that I examined was the conspicuous absence of Christ's ministry within man. Instead of Christ-dependency, the answers offered usually depended upon our own abilities and changed circumstances.

We will find it difficult to trust Christ for change if we don't clearly understand His deity and its implications. Our lack of understanding increases the likelihood of our slipping into the growth deceptions Paul warns us about.

Having briefly examined the relationship of Christ's deity to a life of faith, we are now ready to examine the issue of what Christ has done in the life of the believer as a result of our faith. Specifically Paul says that we have received *fullness* in Christ. Such fullness is the second major reason our faith in Christ works and refers to a significant work that Christ has accomplished within us.

The word "fullness" is a translation of the Greek word *pleroma* which had the usual meaning of completeness and totality. When used in reference to a person, however, *pleroma* implied that the person was filled because he had become all that he was able to become, or to accomplish all that could be accomplished. These definitional foundations enable us to see that Paul is teaching us that we become all we are capable of being and accomplish all we are capable of accomplishing through our faith in Christ. Let's examine this promise more completely.

As we entered into union with Christ at salvation we also entered into a new experience of completeness as people. The One who is the fullness of God lives within us and although we might not understand all that our union with Christ implies, it at least promises that we will discover everything necessary to true fullness as people. In Jesus Christ we lack *nothing* necessary for life and growth and adequacy as people. Notice this truth expressed in the following passages:

> *His divine power has given us everything we need for life and godliness....*
> (2 Peter 1:3)
>
> *Praise be to the God and Father of our Lord Jesus Christ, who has blessed us in the heavenly realms with every spiritual blessing in Christ.*
> (Ephesians 1:3)

When we placed our faith in Jesus Christ, who is the Son of God and the Head over every power and authority, He became our head and power and authority. We no longer need to look to such self-dependent measures as coping, legalism, mysticism, and self-discipline to discover our true potential as people. There is definitely no *substitute* to be found for the precious Son of God and His ministry within our lives and there is clearly no *supplement* necessary to complete His provisions for us.

FAITH AND FULLNESS

A critical question at this juncture pertains to the specifics of our fullness in Christ. What has Christ done for us that has provided such fullness for our lives? Certainly union with Christ is central to the answer and we have already discussed some of what union means and its implications. Paul now turns attention to three additional activities of Christ that occurred when we first believed. These include the creation of a new nature, the bestowing of a new order or quality of life and the granting of forgiveness for our sins. Let's examine each of these in more depth.

> In him you were also circumcised, in the putting off of the sinful nature, not with a circumcision done by the hands of men but with the circumcision done by Christ, having been buried with him in baptism and raised with him through your faith in the power of God, who raised him from the dead. When you were dead in your sins and in the uncircumcision of your sinful nature, God made you alive with Christ. He forgave us all our sins, having canceled the written code, with its regulations, that was against us and that stood opposed to us; he took it away, nailing it to the cross. And having disarmed the powers and authorities, he made a public spectacle of them, triumphing over them by the cross.
> (Colossians 2:11-15)

THE CHANGE FACTOR

CHRIST HAS MADE US NEW PEOPLE

Our study of fullness in Christ begins by examining the nature of man and what changes in man as the result of faith in Christ. When I use the word nature, I am referring to the essential qualities or attributes of an object. For example, the phrase "God's nature" refers to the personality, attributes, and Trinity within the Godhead. Likewise, the phrase "man's nature" refers to the constitutional makeup of man, the essence of what distinguishes man from the rest of creation, the structure or framework of his existence.

There are two Greek words that are usually translated by the word "nature" in English. The most frequent word is *phusis*. In certain contexts, however, the word *sarx* is translated this way and is the word used in Colossians 2. *Sarx* usually is translated "flesh" but can have several different meanings, a fact which has caused untold confusion for many when seeking to understand the Scriptures.

Endless arguments have been held to determine the exact meaning of "flesh" in Scripture. Frustration is inevitable because I believe "flesh" means several different things depending on the context. To force a single meaning on all passages is a distortion of God's Word. A Greek lexicon will show that *sarx* has several meanings, including our nature, our physical body, our human frailty in contrast to God's power, human passions and instinctual drives, and finally our sinful inclinations that tempt us to rebel against God. With such a wide scope of possibilities, the context becomes critical when seeking to understand the meaning of "flesh" in Scripture.

In Colossians 2:11 Paul is using *sarx* in reference to the idea of human nature, as a synonym for *phusis*. His use parallels the ideas in 3:5, 9 of "earthly nature" and "old self." The bottom line of this rather technical discussion is to show that God does something significant to our very nature when we receive Christ as our Savior. He has changed us at the very core of our being.

Our old, sinful nature is that set of characteristics we received from our participation in the human race. Our essence, or constitutional makeup, was inherited from Adam, the progenitor of the human race. Unfortunately, we received from Adam a mixed bag of inheritance. We not only received those things of Adam's that God created, but we also received those things that were inseparably linked to humanity because of Adam's sin and subsequent fall.

In other words, apart from Christ, the nature of man is no longer completely what God intended in Creation, but rather is a distortion caused by sin and the Fall. Man's basic nature is *sinful* in its very essence. This means it is man's nature, or inbred tendency, to sin and distort God's intentions for mankind. Notice how C. S. Lewis puts this:

THE CHANGE FACTOR

> *The process [of the fall of Adam] was not, I conceive, comparable to mere deterioration, . . . it was a loss of status as a species. That condition was transmitted by heredity to all later generations. . . . It was the emergence of a new kind of man, a new species, never made by God . . . it was a radical alteration of his constitution.*[1]

I feel it is critical to understand this point regarding man's nature to appreciate better the miracle of new birth in the life of a believer. When seeking to describe the nature of man specifically, we must recognize that man exists with both physical and nonphysical elements. Physically it is man's nature to have a body. We inherited a physical body from Adam that the Bible describes as being fallen. Such a description is not meant to imply that our bodies are sinful, but rather that due to the judgment God carried out against Adam, each of us has a body that is susceptible to frailty, sickness, sin, and death. Therefore, it is obvious that the body we now possess is not what God intended it to be in Creation. As we shall see later, God is going to do something about the problem of a fallen body for the Christian.

The biblical picture of the nonphysical element, or spiritual part, of man's nature is somewhat more complicated and puzzling. The spiritual makeup of man is not presented in the Scriptures with as much precision and clarity as many would desire. Certain words appear to be used interchangeably and therefore are not presenting hard and fast categories. The two words most frequently encountered in the Scripture regarding the nonphysical part of man's nature are *spirit* (Greek *pneuma*) and *soul* (Greek *psyche*). Let's examine these terms.

The soul, or *psyche*, is used to refer to that part of man which is his seat of personhood, or his identity. It is the "I myself" when thinking about ourselves. It is our inward part, the place of origin for our thinking, feeling, and willing. It is the part of our being that continues to exist when our physical body dies. Although we use our bodies and physical senses to express our thoughts and feelings, our soul has an existence independent of these. The words heart and mind are often used in Scripture as a synonym of *psyche*. Although we can understand the fact that we have a soul, there is also a clear limitation in our conceptualization of this nonphysical part of our nature.

Paul presents the soul (*psyche*) of unregenerate man as being spiritually lost and oriented toward sin. As a result of the Fall we were born with a soul that was spiritually dead and inclined toward a lifestyle of self-will and rebellion against God and His ways. As we lived our lives and chose to carry out these inclinations, we became enslaved to such rebellion as a way of life. In other words, we were sinners by nature *and* by choice.

Notice the following verses:

THE CHANGE FACTOR

> *As for you, you were dead in your transgressions and sins, in which you used to live when you followed the ways of this world and of the ruler of the kingdom of the air, the spirit who is now at work in those who are disobedient. All of us also lived among them at one time, gratifying the cravings of our sinful nature and following its desires and thoughts. Like the rest, we were by nature objects of wrath.*
> (Ephesians 2:1–3)
>
> *Jesus replied, "I tell you the truth, everyone who sins is a slave to sin."*
> (John 8:34)

Let's examine the spiritual deadness of our old natures. The word "spirit" (*pneuma*) is used in Scripture to refer to that part of man's spiritual makeup that enables him to interact and fellowship with God. It is that part of our nonphysical makeup that allows the interaction between creature and Creator that God intended when we were created.

The Word of God describes the nature of the unregenerate man as being alienated from God not only due to the innate sinful orientation of the soul (*psyche*), but also because it is spiritually inadequate. The spirit (*pneuma*) is said to be dead, needing to be made alive through a new birth to enable communion with God.

Thus we begin to understand that the predicament of the natural man goes beyond sin's slavery. The natural man faces the impossibility of fellowship with God because of an inoperative spirit. He is dead to God, hopelessly cut off from fellowship, and under condemnation for sin. Not a very glamorous picture of mankind, yet clearly the picture of true lostness God reveals in His Word.

Perhaps one additional comment needs to be made regarding the spirit (*pneuma*). I feel it is impossible to completely separate the spirit from the soul (*psyche*) in the scriptural discussion of man's nonphysical nature. This spirit doesn't exist apart from the soul, yet the soul can exist with a dead spirit. Rather than an independent separate element of man, the spirit refers to that added capability of a redeemed soul to respond to fellowship with God. Quite simply, the unregenerate soul *cannot* respond to fellowship with God. Our soul needs both redemption *and* spiritual regeneration.

In summary, then, the old nature refers to man's basic makeup apart from Christ. Specifically we found that the old nature included a fallen body and a sinful rebellious soul that was spiritually dead, totally separated from God and completely unable to do a thing about it. What then has Christ done in salvation for this pathetic and hopeless condition? It is to this question we are now ready to turn.

Paul begins explaining the answer to the predicament of the old nature by teaching us that Christ circumcised it away. In other words, Christ did something to change the very essence of our makeup. He literally changed the core of our being. Christ solved the inherited problem of spiritual deadness and a natural bent toward sin and rebellion against God. Christ supernaturally pulled us out of the spiritual consequences of Adam's fall, positionally and experientially. In Adam we were dead, but now in Christ we are alive.

> *For as in Adam all die, so in Christ all will be made alive.*
>
> (1 Corinthians 15:22)

> *For if, by the trespass of the one man, death reigned through that one man, how much more will those who receive God's abundant provision of grace and of the gift of righteousness reign in life through the one man, Jesus Christ.*
>
> (Romans 5:17)

Christ changed our very nature because only by so doing could the deepest ally of sin be destroyed. Christ needed to change us in our very natures so that our inbred, natural tendency to sin and rebel against God could be changed. The phrase "put off" means literally to strip away and cast off. This is what Christ has done to our old nature. He has circumcised it away from us. We are no longer who we once were. Our nature has been changed!

Let's examine the use of the word circumcision in this passage. Circumcision literally refers to the act of cutting away the foreskin of a man. In the Old Testament this physical act became the sign of being one of God's covenant people.

FAITH AND FULLNESS

All Jewish males were required to be circumcised in order to be accepted as God's people. It was the sign of God's covenant promises to Abraham (Gen. 17).

In the New Testament God uses the idea of circumcision to teach a critical concept regarding His covenant people. Circumcision is still a sign of God's covenant people, but the act is no longer a physical one. The cutting away takes place in the nonphysical part of man's nature. Jesus Christ circumcises the old nature away and replaces it with a new nature (an issue we will examine presently). This deeper circumcision was prophesied in the Old Testament.

> "The days are coming," declares the LORD, "when I will punish all who are circumcised only in the flesh . . . even the whole house of Israel is uncircumcised in heart."
>
> (Jeremiah 9:25–26)

> The LORD your God will circumcise your hearts and the hearts of your descendants, so that you may love him with all your heart and with all your soul, and live.
>
> (Deuteronomy 30:6)

> A man is not a Jew if he is only one outwardly, nor is circumcision merely outward and physical. No, a man is a Jew if he is one inwardly; and circumcision is circumcision of the heart, by the Spirit, not by the written code.
>
> (Romans 2:28–29)

THE CHANGE FACTOR

Thus Paul explains that we find fullness in Christ first of all because Christ has circumcised our old nature and put it away from us. Although we don't understand all that circumcision has done, at least we know we have been truly changed. Just as circumcision is an irreversible act physically, so the spiritual circumcision of our old nature is irreversible spiritually. The old nature is actually gone! What is permanently removed will not grow back. Such spiritual circumcision has also removed me in a very real sense from Adam's lineage. My new nature is inherited from another. It is to this issue of our new nature that we must now turn.

We find fullness in Christ secondly through the miracle of being given a new nature. When the old nature is gone, circumcised away, we are finally ready for something new. In response to our faith, Christ actually makes us new creations, having new natures. We are changed, different in the very core and essence of our being. Our nature (*phusis*) is different. Notice the following verses:

> *Therefore, if anyone is in Christ, he is a new creation; the old has gone, the new has come!*
> (2 Corinthians 5:17)
>
> *Neither circumcision [physical] nor uncircumcision means anything; what counts is a new creation.*
> (Galatians 6:15)

FAITH AND FULLNESS

Paul describes this work of creation in Colossians by saying that we have been buried and risen to a new life in Christ. The idea of burial reminds us of circumcision. When we placed our faith in Christ as Savior, our old nature died. We were born again spiritually into a new life. Part of the symbolism of baptism is to affirm our dying and raising again to new life in Christ. We are not referring simply to theoretical, or positional, truths by such statements. It isn't simply that God views us differently (He does, of course!), but the promise is that we are actually different.

We have been raised with Christ through our faith. This truth is not intended by God to be abstract or mystical. Practically, God has given us a new nature in Christ. We are new creatures and as such our life is intended to be different. As we have seen, our old life, our old nature, was at odds with God and tended toward rebellion.

Our new life, our new nature, is reconciled with God and tends toward love and surrender.

The scenario of our natures has changed in the following fashion. Prior to our knowing Christ as Savior it was our nature to rebel against God, to sin and live contrary to His Word. Yet it was possible at times to seek after God and forgiveness. After faith in Christ it is our new nature to love God and to live in harmony with His commands. Yet it is possible at times to rebel. Because of a changed nature, we would have to live contrary to our nature (true misery) to live in rebellion against God and out of the center of His will. A Christian, even though he is a new creation, can make such a foolhardy choice, yet it will always be contrary to his nature to do so.

As we already discussed, our old nature was the result of our inheritance from Adam. We traced our lineage to him. Our new nature, however, traces its lineage to another. Our new nature is created by God and reflects Christ, the Second Adam. He is the firstborn, the progenitor of a new humanity, created to reflect His glory and power.

In addition to escaping the condemnation that was our inheritance from Adam, we have also escaped the spiritual deadness of his nature through our new birth. This new humanity with recovered potential was critical in God's overall redemption of man.

Scripture clearly teaches that when we received Christ we became new creations. Our new birth has given us a new nature. John describes this as receiving the seed of God in 1 John 3:9. The word "seed" is a translation of the Greek word *sperma*, which connotes the ideas of species and order. This is not saying we become God's but rather that we are of a new seed, different from Adam's. God has carried out a creative work within us that has delivered us from Adam's lineage and placed us in the line of Christ. We will grow to resemble the one whose seed we are. Notice these verses:

FAITH AND FULLNESS

> *Put on the new self, which is being renewed in knowledge in the image of its Creator.*
> (Colossians 3:10)
>
> *Put on the new self, created to be like God in true righteousness and holiness.*
> (Ephesians 4:24)

The gift of a new nature has also broken our enslavement to sin. To understand why, let's examine the elements of difference between our old and new natures. As we already examined, our nature (*phusis*) has a physical part and a nonphysical part. Salvation has radically altered our nature, yet there remains a clear continuity between the past and present.

This continuity is the reason why sin remains a problem, as we shall examine in the next chapter. Part of this continuity is seen in the fact that the physical part of our nature has remained the same after salvation. We don't look any different than before. As far as the world is concerned we are still the same. The radical change has occurred in the nonphysical part of us. This explains why the world tends to miss the reality of our new nature. We still exist in fallen bodies susceptible to frailty, sickness, death, and sin. Salvation will eventually bring a change on this level as well, but for now we live with the limitations of a fallen body.

It is the nonphysical, or spiritual, part of our nature where the change has occurred. We are truly different. First of all, our spirit

THE CHANGE FACTOR

(*pneuma*) is now alive, born again at salvation. As we already saw the *pneuma* is that part of man's nature that enables him to interact and fellowship with God. Salvation has given us life in our spirit. We are finally able to fellowship with God. Our fellowship with God is rooted in this miracle, not only in the positional act of justification due to our faith. We can fellowship and live in mystical union with Christ because our spirit is now alive.

As I already explained, the spirit (*pneuma*) cannot be adequately understood if viewed as a separate element from the soul (*psyche*). Instead the spirit is that dimension of our soul that gives us the capability of fellowship with God. The soul can exist with a dead spirit, but the spirit has no existence apart from the soul. Thus we can begin to understand how salvation has radically transformed our souls (*psyche*). Let's examine in more detail this transformation.

The soul is the seat of our personhood, the center of our identity, existence, and basic orientation to life. Our most foundational inclinations have their origin here. As I have said, the brain and body give expression to our feeling and thinking, yet our soul remains deeper than the physical. The old nature's soul was inherited from Adam and was hopelessly rebellious against God. The deepest thoughts and intents of the person were thus corrupted and under condemnation. Christ has made us new creations, that love God and desire obedience at the level of our soul. Such a radical change is Paul's point in the following verse and has tremendous implications for our personality.

In my inner being I delight in God's law.
(Romans 7:22)

Paul is saying that rebellion no longer originates in our nature, or innermost self. This astounding truth is repeated by Peter, who says that sinful desires now war against our souls (1 Peter 2:11). Because of a new nature, the soul is no longer the origin of such sinful impulses. All this is true because we are new creations in Christ.

Our slavery to sin as non-Christians was rooted both in our core spiritual deadness—that is, old natures—and in the choices of sin that inevitably made us sinners by habit. Habits of sinful behavior could never be adequately overcome until we had a change in our hearts that would oppose the impulse to sin. A change in our nature allows spiritually alive souls to begin to affect our mental programming and physical behaviors. The specifics of such change will be covered later.

In summary, the first reason faith in Christ produces fullness, or completeness, is because Christ has raised us to life as new creations, with a definitely changed nature. He circumcised away the old man we once were, with natures inherited from Adam, and has created a new man in its place, with new natures inherited from Christ, the Second Adam, the firstborn of a new humanity. Two more reasons for faith-created fullness remain to be covered and that will be done in the next chapter.

NOTES

1. C. S. Lewis, *The Problem of Pain* (New York: Macmillan, 1948), 70–71.

◆ SIX ◆

Faith and Sin

We have just been examining the meaning of the phrase "fullness [*pleroma*] in Christ" which Paul teaches is the privilege of those who live by faith in Christ, following the formula "live as you received." This promise of such fullness grows out of three key works that Christ has accomplished in our life. The first work, being made new creations, has already been examined. The second and third reasons for fullness can now be developed.

> *When you were dead in your sins and in the uncircumcision of your sinful nature, God made you alive with Christ.*
> (Colossians 2:13)

THE CHANGE FACTOR

FAITH AND REAL LIFE

When we responded to the gospel with faith in Christ, God did something that affected the very experience of what life means for the believer. In Christ, for the first time, we became truly alive at last. The word "life" in the Scriptures is used to refer to two distinctively different concepts. First, it can refer to the concept of mere biological existence. Something has "life" in contrast with something being physically dead. Normally, however, the word "life" in the Scriptures refers to the concept of the *quality* of existence. This concept of "life" is very similar to the idea behind much advertising which challenges us to really "live," grabbing for all the gusto life can offer. Paul is referring to this second concept of "life" in Colossians 2:13.

In addition to giving us a new nature, Jesus Christ, has also granted us the gift of a new quality of existence. He came to make us alive at last, to enable us to begin to know the quality of existence for which God originally created man. The deadness of sin was not limited only to the spiritual aspects of existence, but went beyond this to our total experience of living in this world. It was fullness on this total life level that Christ is promising men. Notice the following verses:

> *I have come that they may have life, and have it to the full.*
>
> (John 10:10)

FAITH AND SIN

> "I am the way and the truth and the life."
> (John 14:6)

> And this is the testimony: God has given us eternal life, and this life is in his Son. He who has the Son has life; he who does not have the Son of God does not have life.
> (1 John 5:11–12)

Eternal life is not limited simply to the promise of a future in heaven with the Lord. Rather, eternal life is the idea of living contrasted with the idea of merely existing. This distinction is necessary when we remember it is not only the saved who continue to exist beyond the death of the physical body. All of mankind possesses a type of continued existence. The difference between mankind has to do with the *quality* of existence. Eternal existence cut off from fellowship with God and without hope for being what we were created to be is the true contrast between eternal life for the believer and eternal damnation. The believer experiences the benefit of eternal fellowship with God, with all of its attendant blessings and fullness.

Such eternal life as I have been describing is presented in the Scriptures as *present* possession of the believer. This eternal life begins the moment we place our faith in Christ as Savior. Such life, as we have seen, is not simply the promise of a future and a hope, but also the promise of a new quality of existence, a true fullness of life. Such life begins *now* and continues beyond our physical death. It is life as God intended life to be. It is the *quality* of existence in which we can live spiritually alive, in fellowship and union with Christ. It is the quality of existence in which the very core of our being, loves God and desires His will. It is the quality of existence in which we can discover a new power to enable us to live victoriously in the midst of a fallen world. It is the quality of existence limited to those who have given new natures.

The promise of "life" so frequently presented in the pages of the New Testament, must be understood in this light. Otherwise we will be tempted to relegate such promises to the dusty storage room labeled "positional truth." In point of fact our faith *has* resulted in critical changes in our position in God's eyes, not the least of which is the promise of justification, or right standing in God's eyes. Such positional truth is a precious birthright of the believer, yet don't overlook the experiential realities God intends to be ours as His children. To do so would be a disservice to God's Word.

Our new life in Christ is indeed life at its fullest. In Christ we discover meaning and purpose for our existence. We find fellowship with God through relationship with Christ and discover the satisfaction of lasting love and acceptance with Him. We begin to discover growth and fruitfulness as we live in conscious dependency upon Christ, a fact that gives great joy to our hearts. Christ truly makes a difference because he gives us *life*, a gift the Father entrusts to His Son for us.

> "I tell you the truth, a time is coming and has now come when the dead will hear the voice of the Son of God and those who hear will live. For as the Father has life in himself, so he has granted the Son to have life in himself."
> (John 5:25–26)

FAITH AND FORGIVENESS

We have seen that faith in Christ gives us fullness as people due to His work of making us new creations and the act of bestowing a new quality of life, eternal life, into His regenerate children. The third reason for fullness is the relationship between faith and forgiveness. Notice the following verses:

> He forgave us all our sins, having canceled the written code, with its regulations, that was against us and that stood opposed to us; he took it away, nailing it to the cross. And having disarmed the powers and authorities, he made a public spectacle of them, triumphing over them by the cross.
> (Colossians 2:13–15)

The third reason we find fullness through faith is because something has been done to deal with the true moral corruption and guilt of our sin. Something has been done to pay for sin and provide forgiveness for those who seek it through repentance and faith in Christ. Fullness is possible because we are truly forgiven people. Let's examine how this forgiveness was accomplished and how it relates to the issue of fullness.

We were dead spiritually as non-Christians. We were cut off from God, having no relationship with Him. Our spiritual deadness had two dimensions to it. First, we were dead because we had a fallen nature that couldn't relate to God even if we wanted it to. We needed a new nature to have the spiritual capability to respond to God. Only then could we worship God in spirit and truth. Second, we were also cut off from Him in practice because we were a morally fallen people. We were a people who sinned as a way of life. These two dimensions created our deadness, a deadness that led to being separated from God.

The cross provided the answer to that deadness of man. Through the work of Christ true forgiveness is available to us. True forgiveness lays at the base of all the workings of God in the life of a person. Our new nature and new life could never have happened apart from the fact that Christ had done something enabling God to forgive us. Then and only then would God go on to other ministries within us.

The cross is the foundation on which true change is built because it is the basis on which God now deals with us as people. Paul goes on

FAITH AND SIN

to explain that the written code against us was canceled. The written code refers to God's revealed laws. Since we are all sinners, we stand condemned according to these laws. The laws of God were broken and that demanded our death. We were a helplessly dying and lost people. But the demands of this code were canceled for the believer, nailed to the cross. Christ fulfilled the demands of the code in Himself. We were reconciled to God permanently. As a result we are now able to benefit from relationship with Christ. We can truly be alive today because we are a forgiven people.

It is only as we live a life built on our understanding of being a forgiven people that we will have confidence to trust in Christ for change and growth. To the degree that we lose sight of the significance of the cross in achieving forgiveness, we will flounder around with guilt-inspired uncertainty, doubting that God will be willing to help us. To the extent that we become a people who do not live appropriating the benefits of such forgiveness through confessing sin when we stumble, we will hesitate to come to God for help. Our spiritual growth is built on the positional realities of forgiveness. It is only as we understand the reality of being a forgiven person that vitality of life and appropriation of power can take place.

This is why we spend time thinking about forgiveness when we share together as believers in the Lord's Supper. Forgiveness lies at the base of our salvation, but also at the base of our growth. At all points of our growth, it's the work that Christ did for us at the cross upon which everything rests. Christ can live within us and can raise us to newness of life through His power because we are forgiven. Due to forgiveness we are a new and alive people, having a new nature within. Morally we can find power through the indwelling Christ to overcome sin as a way of life. We also now have the possibility of experiencing forgiveness as a way of life. We are indeed living in fullness when we have faith in Christ.

SO WHY IS SIN STILL A PROBLEM?

We have looked at the foundational truths regarding change in our lives. We have discovered that faith in Christ, living as we received, is the key factor in personal growth and transformation. We have seen that such faith is practical because Jesus Christ is God and has given us true fullness as people. This fullness results from Christ's work of making us new creations, of bestowing upon us eternal life and of granting us true forgiveness. In light of such remarkable works, why do we still have problems with sin? It is the answer to this question to which we will now turn.

CHANGE MUST MOVE FROM CORE TO CRUST

Sin continues to be a problem in the Christian life because there is a process involved in allowing our new nature to affect our actions and attitudes. To understand this fact we must review our model of man.

When we became a Christian, Christ changed the very core of our being. We were made new creations. Our soul was saved and made spiritually alive. We now loved God and desired His will at the core of our true selves. Unfortunately such a change, although real, did not immediately lead to a total change in our personalities. It merely set up the conditions for change to begin to occur.

Our personality is not synonymous with our innermost being, or soul. Rather, our personality refers to that set of characteristic ways of thinking, feeling, and behaving that has come to mark our lives. Our personalities are the behavioral imprintings in our brains that are the outgrowth of the interplay between our soul, the life circumstances we have faced, and the choices we make over time. We are creatures of habit in our thinking, feeling, and behavior. In a sense, the personality bridges the gap between the physical and immaterial parts of man, reflecting something of both our nature, choices, and life environment. Personality is the programming that controls life responses.

When we become a Christian, one of the key factors contributing to our personalities in the present is finally changed. In receiving a new nature, our soul is changed and our spirit is reborn. Thus the core of our being begins send-

THE CHANGE FACTOR

ing a different set of signals to our minds, signals to love God and obey His commands. Such signals run counter to the habit patterns of our personalities. Something must be done to reprogram our personalities to think, feel, and act in accord with our new hearts. Change must move from our core to our crust.

As you can see, the old nature has a significant role in creating our personalities in the present. Our old nature continues to haunt us throughout our lives due to this programming, or imprinting, in our brains. This explains the reluctance many feel to actually accept the fact that the old nature is dead and gone. Because they see this current effect of the old nature they conclude it is alive and well. We must recognize its death however, so we can see the battle ground is in our programming and *not* in our nature.

Personality change is a *process*. It is only when we live by faith in Christ, looking to Him to provide the enablement, that we will see our characteristic ways of thinking, feeling, and behaving gradually being conformed to the image of Christ. Such mind renewal, or programming, is the focal point of growth. Notice how the following verses put this problem:

> *You were taught, with regard to your former way of life, to put off your old self, which is being corrupted by its deceitful desires; to be made new in the attitude of your minds; and to put*

on the new self, created to be like God in true righteousness and holiness.
(Ephesians 4:22–24)

Do not conform any longer to the pattern of this world, but be transformed by the renewing of your mind.
(Romans 12:2)

Each Christian discovers an ongoing struggle with the temptation from his preprogrammed personality to live like he once lived. Each Christian also finds himself living with a fallen physical body that responds to sinful inclinations and temptations. Although our physical body is not inherently sinful, it does respond to sinful temptations that constantly assail it. Sin remains a problem for the believer because we still possess fallen bodies and programmed personalities. Through union with Christ we discover the resources of power to combat the temptations inevitable in our condition.

WE STILL LIVE IN A FALLEN WORLD

Sin also remains a problem for the believer because God has left us to exist in a fallen world. We will face the struggle of temptation as the world seeks to squeeze us into its mold. The world system around us does not act to foster righteousness and obedience to God because it is the product of Satan and not God. We will find a constant adversary appealing to our past programming in our personalities, calling for resources that only God can give to maintain victory.

THE CHANGE FACTOR

GOD REQUIRES OUR COOPERATION

The third reason sin remains a problem is that God intends for us to do something to cooperate with the change process. We can never change in our own strength. Christ must do that which is impossible for us to do on our own. Yet the Scripture is clear that God *demands* that we do what lies within the realm of our ability if true growth is ever to be achieved. We most definitely have a role.

We now can begin to understand the paradox at the beginning of this book. Paul says he works with all of God's power. It is the apparent paradox of "I do" and "God does." God does what we cannot do, that is, He changes our hearts and gives us power to overcome sin. We must do our part by choosing to live in obedience and dependency. Our role can be summarized by the words *trust* and *obey*.

We are called upon to trust in Christ's power to enable us to grow and deal with sin. This is the essence of faith in Christ and is necessary because God chose not to impart inherent power to His children. We are intended to live a life of dependency upon Christ. However, God also calls upon us to *choose* to live in obedience to Him. We choose to act obediently and then trust in Christ's enablement to carry out our choice. Faith was never intended to be separated from obedience. We were not called to a passive life as believers. Sin will never be overcome in practice until we act in obedience to counter its influence in our bodies and personalities.

We are to be obedient as a way of life. We are called to be obedient in our feelings, thinking, and behavior. It is the practical question of obedience in these areas to which we now are ready to turn.

◆ SEVEN ◆

Obeying in Our Hearts and Minds

> *Since, then, you have been raised with Christ, set your hearts on things above, where Christ is seated at the right hand of God. Set your minds on things above, not on earthly things. For you died, and your life is now hidden with Christ in God. When Christ, who is your life, appears, then you also will appear with him in glory.*
> (Colossians 3:1–4)

In these opening verses of Colossians 3, Paul provides the transition to our role in the study of change. He begins by reminding us that we are indeed a resurrected people. As an outcome of faith in Christ, we are no longer dead, but alive, risen to a new quality of life altogether with Christ. Through faith we have been changed at the very core of our being and now have every potential for transformation in our personalities due to the power and life of the risen Christ alive within us. We are also in union with Jesus Christ as a result of the working of the Holy Spirit of God. As a result of these miracles the stage is set for developing our role in personality change.

I briefly summarized our role in change at the end of the previous chapter. Basically God commands us to *trust* and *obey*. We are called to *trust* Christ to provide our strength for living life in this world. By faith we are to rest in the assurance of His promises of life, new birth, and enablement. In short, we are to "live as we received" (God's formula for change). Yet we are also called upon to *obey* as the second element of our role. Let's now examine this second element in greater depth.

The relationship of obedience to change is critical to understand. Reflecting on the truths of Colossians 2 inevitably leads to an attitude of praise and thanksgiving before the Lord. But once you get down from the mountaintop and begin to look at your life in this fallen world, it is easy to become discouraged and wonder how these tremendous truths really start to relate today where you are living. It is at this very point where Christians often encounter the most problems. The real biblical principle of change is impossible to understand apart from the truths clarified in Colossians 2. But the principles would be equally impossible to apply apart from the truths explained in Colossians 3.

OBEYING IN OUR HEARTS AND MINDS

As I mentioned already, if one were to begin studying chapter 3 without first understanding the foundational principles in chapter 2, there would be a strong chance of misunderstanding God's intentions. Chapter 3 could easily become the basis for trusting in self-disciplines to obey the commands of God's Word. Without understanding our true powerlessness apart from Christ, an issue well developed in Colossians 2, we most certainly could fall into such a trap. God had good reasons for putting chapter 2 before chapter 3. It is crucial we follow His inspired contextual development. Having done this we are capable of now understanding our role in Christian living.

How are we to understand the relationship between obedience and growth? Often when people start to understand the truths that are talked about in Colossians 2 they conclude our role is simply to sit back and wait for God to do something. This results in equating our role with passivity.

Actually, we have a very important role in change. God clearly states our responsibility in the process of achieving transformation in our minds, emotions, and behaviors. God intends through our cooperation to allow our personality to increasingly reflect our new nature. There is definitely a role we are to play in change, a role for our mind, a role for our emotions, and a role for our will. All three areas have a function in achieving the transformation that God desires to see in our life and personality. Although it is true that we don't have power in ourselves to carry out such transformation, we most definitely have a role.

SETTING OUR HEARTS

We begin our role by setting our hearts on things that are above. Grammatically this phrase is a present imperative, an ongoing command, a day-to-day responsibility. It is not enough to "set your heart on things above" every Sunday. Rather, it is a command to make setting your heart on things above the focus of your total life. The word "setting" is a translation of a Greek word meaning to desire to seek after, to constantly strive after. When Paul uses the word "heart" in this passage he is referring to our emotions, desires, and longings.

As we all have discovered, emotions can be affected by more than our new nature. External circumstances and physiological conditions also have an effect. In spite of such frustrating vulnerability, the fact remains that our emotions can be very responsive to our new nature in Jesus Christ. God is saying we need to make choices to allow our new nature to start having an effect on our emotions. We do so in the following ways:

1. Be Vulnerable With God. We begin obeying by choosing to put ourselves in places where we are emotionally vulnerable to God. God will minister to us at an emotional level in several key areas. First, we must choose to have consistent devotions. Quiet times of prayer and Bible study before the Lord create an environment that God utilizes to allow emotional healing to pervade our personalities. Such devotional times provide needed emotional refreshment and revitalization.

Second, we are to choose to be consistent in attending times of corporate worship. Often God's Spirit chooses to use times of worship to lift our hearts, restore our joy, and renew our enthusiasm for living. All of us have had this blessed experience and can attest to the importance worship has to our emotional well-being. Yet when we are emotionally down, it is usually in devotions and worship where we slip out of consistency as people. Our obedience here is critical to emotional health and transformation.

Third, it is important to choose to listen to Christian music and read quality, edifying Christian literature. Such vehicles are important in helping us become emotionally vulnerable to God. Recognize, however, that *we* must choose to obey the Lord in such areas of emotional vulnerability.

2. Meditate Upon Kingdom Realities. We next become obedient to the command to set our hearts by hungering for spiritual reality and allowing our heart to seek for the Lord. In other words, we are to choose to allow our emotions to be affected by heavenly things, instead of simply earthly things. We can't totally stop being affected by earthly things as long as we live in this world, but we can start to make choices that will allow us also to be affected by things that are above. We must hunger and thirst deep within for the righteousness that is ours in Christ. We should long for the holiness that is now possible in our lives due to what Christ has already done. We can long for the lifestyle we see in the risen Christ as He is seated at the right hand of God. Long for deeper friendship and relationship with Jesus Christ. Long for the father-child relationship with the Father that is now possible for us because of what Christ has accomplished on our behalf. He is at the right hand of the Father, constantly there interceding for us, making forgiveness a moment-by-moment reality in our relationship with God. We should meditate on such truths.

There definitely is a role for our emotions in the Christian life. Although emotions can be deceptive due to the fact they are so quickly affected by the fallen world in which we live, we must never come to the point of disregarding emotions entirely because they can so easily mislead us. God is definitely interested in transforming our emotions and requires us to be obedient in our heart's focus. God wants our hearts to long for Jesus and the realities that He shares in His Word. Will you choose to allow your emotions to be affected?

OBEYING IN OUR HEARTS AND MINDS

"For where your treasure is, there your heart will be also."
(Matthew 6:21)

It is a sobering thing for us to discover what it is our hearts long for the most. What is your treasure, that which affects your heart the most? Is it spiritual things? Is it the knowledge of what Christ has done and is doing? Is it the knowledge of your future and your hope? Is it the knowledge of His promises in the present? Whatever it is that most deeply affects you will clearly show where your heart is set. Such an evaluation will tell you very quickly whether you are setting your heart on this world, or on eternal things at the right hand of God the Father.

The Christian life isn't simply a matter of sitting passively back and waiting for God to do something. There is a role for the exercise of our new nature. We are to begin such a role by setting our hearts through being vulnerable to God and meditating upon kingdom truths.

SETTING OUR MINDS

Paul continues his discussion of our role in change by next turning attention to the mind. He teaches that we are responsible to set our minds on the truths of God's Word. We must think about the promises and realities discovered in the Scriptures.

This is an exercise that we must determine

THE CHANGE FACTOR

to carry out. God will not do it for us. God calls for an active response in our minds. We have an active role in setting our minds. We have an ongoing responsibility to consciously reflect upon the truths of chapter 2 as a habit of life. If you wait for difficult times to occur to begin to set your mind on these truths it will be too late. It is necessary to habitualize the realization of these truths and set our minds on them.

The particular phrase "setting the mind" comes from the Greek word *phroneo*, which means to direct your thinking, or think deeply about something. The idea is to give a focus to our minds. Determine to think about the right things; don't wait until you feel like it. Setting our minds is an exercise of the new man. Since we live in a fallen body and a fallen world, we will inevitably face influences that will try to keep our new nature from controlling your mind. Our new nature wants to think about the right things, but we need to act obediently upon these inclinations. This is something we can and must do. Paul affirms this point in the following verse:

> *Finally, brothers, whatever is true, whatever is noble, whatever is right, whatever is pure, whatever is lovely, whatever is admirable—if anything is excellent or praiseworthy—think about such things.*
>
> (Philippians 4:8)

OBEYING IN OUR HEARTS AND MINDS

God commands us in Colossians 3 to think about the things that are above, truths that are based on revelation, not sight. We need to break out of our tunnel vision and realize that there are realities beyond our sensual awareness. We are to set our minds on things above, not earthly things, especially in issues of change. We are to set our minds on God's answers, not the world's. The world's answers may seem to make sense and have an appearance of wisdom, but they are not founded in the things above, in the truths of the Word. We need to allow our minds to set on things that transcend the world and depend on the reality of revelation from God in His Word. Paul specifically challenges us to focus our minds on the following truths:

1. *Our New Life in Christ.* First of all, we are supposed to think about what has happened to us as a result of faith in Christ. We have died and our old sin nature is gone. Sin no longer has to be our master. We have a new nature, yet the old nature had a lot of years to affect the programming of our personality. We are constantly fighting against just such programming. Problem attitudes and actions are often rooted in our former manner of life. When the old programming exerts itself, realize the problem isn't the deepest level of who we are. Instead, it is the old programming that is the problem. We need to realize that we truly have died, but our death has not erased off the scene the effects of our former life.

We are a new creation in the core of our being. Satan will try to convince us that this is not true, but God says to set our minds on the truth. The truth is that we have a new nature and the deepest level of our life is allied with God rather than allied with sin.

2. Our Protection in Christ. Second, we are to set our minds on our protection. Our new life is hidden with Christ in God. Our new nature is a spiritual reality. Our outer body doesn't look transformed because it hasn't been. It is still the same. But there has been a change in the inner man. This change in the inner man is now safely hidden with Christ.

The key implication of this truth is the assurance that sin cannot affect or pervert the new nature. The new nature is hidden safely with Christ in living union with Him. Our personality can still be affected due to sin choices, but our new nature will never be corrupted because it is hidden in Christ. You will always be a new creation in mystical union with Jesus Christ.

3. Our Power in Christ. The third issue upon which we are to set our minds is the source of our power for living in this world. We are a protected people, but we are also a powerless people. Our new nature is impotent, powerless on its own to deal with sin and keep our bodies under control. Notice how Paul expresses this impotency in Romans:

OBEYING IN OUR HEARTS AND MINDS

> *For in my inner being I delight in God's law; but I see another law at work in the members of my body, waging war against the law of my mind and making me a prisoner of the law of sin at work within my members. What a wretched man I am! Who will rescue me from this body of death? Thanks be to God—through Jesus Christ our Lord!*
> (Romans 7:22–25)

Sooner or later we must come to Paul's conclusion about our lives. We must recognize that our new nature is powerless on its own to deal with the war against the law of sin at work in our physical bodies. Sin attacks us, tempting us through our senses, our old programming, the environment of the world around us, and through Satan. We need strength beyond our new nature to successfully combat such temptations. That is exactly what we have in Jesus Christ.

> *I have been crucified with Christ, and I no longer live, but Christ lives in me. The life I live in the body I live by faith in the Son of God.*
> (Galatians 2:20)

> *I can do everything through him who gives me strength.*
> (Philippians 4:13)

Jesus Christ is the power and strength of our life in this world. Jesus Christ lives His life through the power of the Holy Spirit in a yielded believer, providing the strength the new nature lacks to deal with sin. When I say we are to be dependent on the strength that Christ provides, the life of Christ living through us, I do not mean that somehow Christ displaces our new nature, or our personality. Christ doesn't take the place of our personality. We are not challenged to cease to exist, becoming like a robot for God to live through. That is not the picture or the meaning of spiritual life.

God is not trying to abolish us as human beings and have Jesus Christ replace us. God's goal is to restore us to our true potential so that we can become a vehicle through which God can express Himself. Therefore He doesn't abolish our personality, He purifies and empowers it through the indwelling Christ to enable us to be what He created us to be. Redemption at the cross recovered man, it did not replace man.

Therein is a misunderstanding that often arises when seeking to understand the spiritual life and what it means to let Christ live through us. Christ will not work in a way that ultimately does away with mankind. We are powerless in ourselves, but we are still a redeemed people. God so desired to fellowship with us that He sent His only Son to die on our behalf. He did not die on the cross to create a race of robots. Christ died on the cross to create a race of people who choose to love and follow God. People who choose, knowing the conditions that we live under in this world, to let Christ live through them. We are not people called to cease to exist.

When God commands us not to let "self" live or to "die to ourselves," it is a dual challenge. First, it is a challenge not to let sin take control through the old programming that is in our body. Second, it is a challenge not to believe that our new nature has power in itself to somehow carry out righteousness. God never meant this phrase as a challenge to do away with our personality! Our condition of yieldedness is basic to allowing our new nature to mature and renew our personality. The price of our birth was the death of Christ. The price of our growth is our dying to self-reliance and trusting in Christ to enable us to live obediently in this world.

4. *Our Future in Christ.* The fourth issue for our mindset is our future. We have not yet received all the benefits of salvation. Our justification is certain, our ultimate future is assured, our destiny is certain, but the outworking of salvation is not complete. We have been given a new nature in Christ, that is, become new creations in the core of our being. The new nature is affecting our personality in the present through our life of faith and obedience.

Eventually our new nature will include a new physical body. When Christ comes again the whole man that God has sought to redeem will finally be seen. When Christ comes again our new nature will be united with a new body and it will no longer be powerless and impotent to express itself. We will have a new body by which our new nature will be able to express itself naturally and perfectly. That is what the glorification of our body is all about. The end result of justification is glorification. That is our future and hope.

This is part of the significance of the statement that when Christ, who is our life, appears then we also will appear. Right now we are not totally appearing. We are having to live in conscious dependency on the indwelling Christ because our new nature is unable by itself to change our personality or control our physical body. When Christ comes again we will finally appear, completely what God created us to be. We will appear with a new body, a resurrection body like His. This is my future. That is your future. What could be more exciting! The new nature we have now longs to be what God wants it to be, yet groans and is miserable because we see ourselves struggling with weakness. In the future my new nature will unite with a new body that won't have that struggle. That is my destiny.

Part of the purpose of redemption is to bring me a body that is free from sin and the influences of sin. It will be a body that my new nature can control on its own, a body that will act in light of my heart. At that time every aspect of who I am will be able to express my love of God. Part of God's purpose in creation was to have a creature who was able to love and enjoy Him. Redemption's completion at the time of Christ's coming will allow such a purpose to become reality. Our present weakness will be gone forever. What a promise to set our minds on:

> *So will it be with the resurrection of the dead. The body that is sown is perishable, it is raised imperishable; it is sown in dishonor, it is raised in glory; it is sown in weakness, it is raised in power; it is sown a natural body, it is raised a spiritual body . . . just as we have borne the likeness of the earthly man, so shall we bear the likeness of the man from heaven.*
> (1 Corinthians 15:42–44, 49)

This is our destiny, our future, and hope. But for today, we are impotent. Today we do not have the power in ourselves to let our new nature express itself. The power for the new nature to express itself through our bodies and personalities is dependent upon the indwelling Christ. This will always be the case as long as we live in this world. That is the reason that our life has to be constantly lived by faith in the indwelling Christ. Our condition of impotence will never change or be different until redemption is completed at the second coming of Christ.

◆ EIGHT ◆

Obeying in Our Behavior

This chapter concludes the study of our role in the change process. As I have already pointed out, we are powerless in ourselves to carry out the desires of the new nature we received when we were born again. We will always find ourselves unable to align with all of God's will if we are depending upon our own strength to accomplish it. Such a discovery may take years to arrive at, but inevitably we find ourselves face to face with our own inadequacies in serving and following the Lord.

The length of time in arriving at such a conclusion varies depending upon teaching and an individual's inherent strengths and capabilities. Because of such impotence, faith in Christ is critical if we are to discover change in the Christian. In spite of impotence, we are still commanded to obey God's commands. We are to act in obedience while maintaining a Christ-dependency. We have seen how this relates to thinking and emotions. We now must examine how this relates to actual behavior. To do this we must first examine the role of the will in growth.

A FREE WILL

Although we are powerless to carry out the commands of God and desires of our new nature, we are still able to choose to do God's will. Let's examine this apparent paradox. Our chooser, our volition, has been set free in salvation. Our wills are no longer in bondage to sin. The practical result of this is that God can, and does, command us to make choices. He commands us to choose to align with His Word and to trust in His Son. We have already examined such choices in the area of setting our hearts and our minds.

Now we turn attention to the issue of actual behavior. God commands us to choose to align with righteousness and truth, commands which would be meaningless if we are a people with enslaved wills.

The issue at hand involves the exercise of our uniqueness as man, a creature given the right of volition. God created us with the unique ability to make choices, real choices. Part of what makes man different from the rest of God's creation is this volitional ability. Such an ability to choose makes man a truly autonomous creature in this universe. Our life is not dictated by purely instinctual drives, as is the rest of the animal kingdom. What a wondrous creation we are in God's loving designs!

This ability to make choices was rooted in our very creation. It is crucial we don't miss this point. Part of God's intention in creation was to have creatures who could make choices. This was necessary in order for our love and obedience to mean anything to God. He made us able to make choices instead of being preprogrammed. We are not robots who simply respond in a mechanical way to a set of programmed instructions. The source of the greatest glory of man, and also his greatest shame, is his ability to make choices. It is creatures such as this whom God loved—loved enough to send His only Son to die for them.

This affirmation of our ability to choose implies the issue of responsibility. We can choose, yet we must live with the outcomes of our choices. The freedom we enjoy as autonomous creatures carries with it resultant responsibilities. We must answer for the choices we make in this world. For example, think of someone choosing to step out of a window on the top floor of a tall building. A creature of instinct could never make such a choice, because his instinctual drives prevent such foolhardiness.

THE CHANGE FACTOR

We, however, can make such a choice. We are totally free to step out the window, but with such a step our freedom ceases. Other laws act on us as gravity pulls us faster and faster toward disaster on the ground. We might change our mind on the way down, but we can't change the repercussions of our choices.

Such is the two-edged sword of freedom of choices. No freedom of choice truly exists without the resulting responsibility for our choices. For example, Adam and Eve had to decide whether to obey or not to obey God. This was a real choice. Yet the choice of disobedience brought them into inescapable repercussions, which we discussed earlier—that is, the sin nature and spiritual death. They had to answer for their choice, and so have we, ever since. Thus our will is a privilege and a heavy responsibility at the same time.

It is almost paradoxical. We can make real, true choices as a Christian. These choices can lead to victory, growth, and change, or they can lead to defeat and growing unrighteousness. We can make choices and yet we must live with the results of such choices. Our freedom in Christ does not allow escape from such inevitability.

It is important that we recognize that the cross delivers us from a certain sense of answerability for our choices. We first recognize this in the issue of standing. Our faith and repentance has resulted in our being justified in God's eyes, at peace with Him. We now possess forgiveness

OBEYING IN OUR BEHAVIOR

and right standing due to the atoning work of Christ on the cross of Calvary. Our works and actions in the present do not affect our standing and position which is eternally secure in the promises of God. In this sense Christ has provided a way to escape the outcome of our sins.

A second circumstance where we find deliverance from the outcome of past choices has to do with the practical problem of sin. Previous chapters have shown the work of Christ in freeing us from sin's slavery. In spite of past sin choices, Christ has made us new creatures who are delivered from sin's slavery. The issue facing us as free people in Jesus Christ is how we will use this freedom. Our will, or volition, has an important role in maximizing or minimizing the benefits of such deliverance from sin's slavery. We can choose to align with our new nature and live in conscious dependence on the life of Jesus with whom we are in union, or we can choose to indulge the remnants of the old man we once were. Notice the way Paul put this choice to the Galatians:

> You, my brothers, were called to be free. But do not use your freedom to indulge the sinful nature; rather, serve one another in love.... So I say, live by the Spirit, and you will not gratify the desires of the sinful nature.
> (Galatians 5:13, 16)

From such a passage as this it becomes obvious that growing and changing in the Christian life involves the exercise of our wills. Although, as has been shown, we are powerless to carry out the choices made, yet we are not powerless to make choices. As a result, we are commanded to choose, or "will," certain things in our Christian life.

We are to combine these choices with an attitude of confident dependency upon Jesus Christ to become our strength in carrying out the choices made. Thus we are commanded to set our hearts and minds on the Lord, and live in obedience to His commands.

ACTIVE PASSIVITY

Our growth and change reflects the concept of active passivity. We are to be actively setting our hearts, minds, and behavior upon the Lord and His Word. At the same time we are to recognize the powerlessness of our new nature to carry out in life such determinations.

The result is the choice to live in dependent reliance upon the strength of Christ's life living through us to carry out the choices we make. Such perspective of active passivity must be clear to those who desire growth. It is more than simply a mental game. If we make choices that are correct, but trust in our own resources to carry them out, the result will inevitably be failure and frustration. If, however, we recognize our powerlessness and realize that Christ must be our strength, but sit back believing without our active obedience, the result will be just as

OBEYING IN OUR BEHAVIOR

frustrating and just as much a failure. We must keep both truths in delicate balance to maintain the proper mentality of response in Christian living.

In Colossians 3, Paul shows that we are called upon to make two major choices in our day-to-day walk in Christ. First, we must choose not to align with the influences stemming from our old nature and sin's temptations. Second, we must choose to align with our new nature and live in dependency upon the indwelling Christ for power, change, and growth. Such choices are made in a general way each day, as well as specifically as we face the day's unique temptations to rebel against God and His commands. With such a backdrop of understanding the role of the will, we are ready to examine the final portion of Colossians.

> *Put to death, therefore, whatever belongs to your earthly nature: sexual immorality, impurity, lust, evil desires and greed, which is idolatry. Because of these, the wrath of God is coming. You used to walk in these ways, in the life you once lived. But now you must rid yourself of all such things as these: anger, rage, malice, slander, and filthy language from your lips. Do not lie to each other, since you have taken off your old self with its practices and have put on the new self, which is being renewed in knowledge in the image of its Creator. Here there is no Greek or Jew, circumcised or uncircumcised, barbarian, Scythian, slave or free, but Christ is all, and is in all.*
> (Colossians 3:5–11)

THE CHANGE FACTOR

PUT TO DEATH THE OLD LIFESTYLE

The major choices previously identified in a life of obedience are plainly spelled out here. The first aspect of our choice is to put to death what belongs to our old nature. It is both interesting and necessary to notice that we were not commanded to put to death our old nature. The concept that we are somehow responsible to kill our old nature is unbiblical. Such a death is God's responsibility. He accomplished this death when we were born again in the Spirit. We have previously examined how Christ circumcised our old nature away when we were saved. So the issue facing us is not how we are to put to death our old nature, but rather how to put to death what belonged to that old sin nature, those continuing effects in our personality that were habitualized during our past.

The problem we all face is how to deal with the past programming our old nature left in our personalities. This past programming is seeking to assert its control over actions and attitudes in the present. Notice how the Scriptures describe this problem:

> *You were taught, with regard to your former way of life, to put off your old self, which is being corrupted by its deceitful desires; to be made new in the attitude of your minds.*
>
> (Ephesians 4:22–23)
>
> *You used to walk in these ways, in the life you once lived.*
>
> (Colossians 3:7)

OBEYING IN OUR BEHAVIOR

> ... since you have taken off your old self with its practices ...
>
> (Colossians 3:9)

God commands us to put the actions and attitudes, which belonged to our past nature, to death. The Greek word *nekrosate* is used here and literally means to exterminate. The idea is to recognize that such actions and attitudes do not reflect your true self and can be overcome as you live both obediently and in a Christ-dependent manner. Such a life of faith will allow the actions and attitudes to become as dead as the nature that initially programmed them.

Actually, you are dealing with temptation to sin attacking you through your old programming. You are not dealing with your true nature at all. We are not spiritually schizophrenic, battling inside between two natures that are both really us. Rather we are facing a battle between our new nature (the real us) and the temptation to sin attacking through our past programming. It is not nature against nature, but rather new nature against sin and its deceptions.

When I can see that my old nature is truly dead and therefore no longer my problem, I can better trust Christ's power to keep its current effects in my life under control. My role is to determine to be obedient to Christ and no longer indulge the old programming. Notice the following verses:

> Do not use your freedom to indulge the sinful nature.
>
> (Galatians 5:13)
>
> Those who belong to Christ Jesus have crucified the sinful nature with its passions and desires.
>
> (Galatians 5:24)

As we choose to be obedient, we are also to trust the indwelling Christ's power to enable us to carry out our obedience and keep the passions and desires, left behind when the old nature was put away, from controlling our life in the present. Such a choice of obedience and dependence will insure that the old passions cannot capture our body to do their bidding. Apart from the power of the indwelling Christ, our new nature would be powerless to overcome the temptations we face.

Though our old nature is dead and the new nature is alive and living in vital union with Jesus Christ, the warfare will continue between the desires of the new nature and the desires of our old sinful nature's programming. Victory is not seen by the end of temptation and struggle, but rather by the end of defeat. God's grace doesn't remove us from battle, but rather enables us to win the battle when living dependently upon Him.

A word of caution is appropriate at this point. Earlier I stressed that true freedom carries with it responsibilities. We cannot escape the outcome of our choices. The more one chooses to live as if the old nature were alive, giving in to the desires programmed into our brains and bodies, the more we will find ourselves living in defeat and frustration. In Christ we have all the power necessary to put the inclinations of our new nature into control of our body and personality. Christ will not accomplish this, however, apart from our willing it to be so. Remember, we are powerless to carry out the choices made, but we are not powerless to make choices. The Christian life is an obedient life, lived in constant dependency upon the one who alone can strengthen us.

LIVE CONSISTENT WITH WHO YOU ARE

In verse 10 we are told to realize that we have put on a new nature when we received Christ. We are commanded to live consistent with who we really are. We are to choose to allow our new nature to rule over our body and personality through the power of our union with the indwelling Christ. Basically this means to allow the "inner you" to become the "real you," shining through your body and personality. We are to live up to our new potential as new creations in Jesus Christ. What exactly is this potential?

Just as a seed sprouts and grows into a plant, our new nature is being built up into the very image of its source, Jesus Christ. Such growth is expressed in the area of our personality. As our new nature grows and is manifested increasingly in our life, our personalities will be drawn more and more into conformity to Jesus Christ.

Our new nature is like a seed that has sprouted and is beginning to grow. We know already what we will end up looking like. A seed will turn into what created it. A corn seed won't turn into a bean plant and a bean plant won't turn into a tomato. The variable in the process is not the end result, but rather the time involved in growth. We can certainly make choices that hinder the growth of our new nature and its expression in our personalities, but we can't change the essence of our new nature. Notice how Paul puts it.

> *Put on the new self, which is being renewed in knowledge in the image of its Creator.*
> (Colossians 3:10)
>
> *And we, who with unveiled faces all reflect the Lord's glory, are being transformed into his likeness with ever-increasing glory, which comes from the Lord, who is the Spirit.*
> (2 Corinthians 3:18)

This then is the process of growth and change. It involves both God and ourselves. God does the changing and growing, we do the willing and trusting. Notice how delicate is this balance. We are called to believe the tremendous truths of what is ours in Christ Jesus. We are to set our hearts, minds and wills upon Him. Then we are to trust in our union with Christ to provide the strength to accomplish what we are powerless to do on our own. Such a balance of obedience and trusting dependence on Christ will produce the change and growth that is honoring to God and is the deepest desire of our hearts. May God enable you the reader to find the alternative to coping through the discovery of Christ as your life.

> *Love the Lord your God with all your heart and with all your soul and with all your strength.*
> (Deuteronomy 6:5)